T0032973

MORE PRAISE FOR

The
Newlyweds

"*The Newlyweds* is stunning. It's a sharp and moving explora-
tion of the relationships of three embattled couples; the writing is
beautiful and the storytelling blindingly clear. Mansi Choksi looks
at love in modern India with the appealing perspective of both a
knowing insider, and a curious, wary outsider. The result is an
intimate story of India, and of the perils and pleasures of love, like
no other."

—Alexis Okeowo, *New Yorker* staff writer, and author of
*A Moonless, Starless Sky: Ordinary Women and Men
Fighting Extremism in Africa*

"[Choksi] skillfully uses these human stories to highlight the dangerous trajectory of Hindu fundamentalism under the regime of
current Prime Minister Narendra Modi. Her descriptions are rife
with detail and, at times, truly lyrical. A moving and largely well-
reported account of love in modern India."

—*Kirkus Reviews*

"Choksi debuts with an engrossing study of traditional matchmaking and modern youth in India. She fluidly traces the path each couple navigated from parental home to independence and persuasively analyzes the economic, religious, and cultural stresses they endured. This is a heart-wrenching and inspiring portrait of love under pressure."

—*Publishers Weekly*

"Choksi's narrative structure braids [her subjects' strands] cleverly so that, as the stakes keep rising, the tension escalates through cinematic jumps and cuts. Her scenes are alive with singular details, vivid language and crisp dialogue. The net effect is that we become so vested in the lives of these six people—and the collateral damage they leave in their wake—that they linger with us long after reading."

—*The Star Tribune*

"An interesting and highly readable examination of the complexities and intersections of love, marriage, and tradition in India."

—*Library Journal*

"Love is transformative, even when it fails. That is one of the lessons of *The Newlyweds*. And just as it is with love, I felt most alive when reading this book."

—Amitava Kumar, author of
A Time Outside This Time

"A profound book on the politics of love, of couples who brave everything and everyone to be together. Told with warmth, truth, and humanity, Mansi Choksi's *The Newlyweds* is an extraordinary look at what it takes to be together in modern India."

—Nikesh Shukla, author of *Brown Baby*

"If you believe in great love stories, read Mansi Choksi's *The Newlyweds*. In this exemplary work of narrative nonfiction, Choksi follows three Indian couples for six years to bring us the most nuanced, lyrical, and moving book about love and marriage in modern India yet written. Essential reading for anyone seeking to understand youth in India today—or for anyone who believes in the galactic powers of love to change history, personal and political."

—Suketu Mehta, author of
Maximum City: Bombay Lost and Found

"A work of investigative reportage written in a vivid literary style, exploring the complex themes of inter-faith, inter-caste and same-sex marriages in the cities and villages of India."

—*IndiaCurrents*

"A work of non-fiction, but written with such literary flair that you wonder whether the photos of the protagonists are a double bluff and it really is a novel after all."

—*New Humanist*

"This is a startlingly good book. The meticulously reported stories of three couples–and the social forces that stand in their way–are intimate, revelatory, and as gripping as a novel. I couldn't put it down."

—Samira Shackle, author of
Karachi Vice: Life and Death in a Contested City

"Mansi Choksi's rigorously reported, beautifully written debut signals the arrival of a major new voice in nonfiction."

—Sonia Faleiro, author of *The Good Girls*

"A rare insight into modern love in India . . . astonishing and unforgettable . . . a vibrant observer whose ability lies in capturing the subtleties of life in a way that's nuanced and purposeful."

—*The New Arab*

"I found The Newlyweds compelling, and sometimes heartbreaking, because Choksi followed the couples' stories beyond happy endings. In a country where two out of every three people are under the age of 35, and where marriage is often presented as an inescapable familial duty for young women, the simple act of choosing to fall in love has radical repercussions for the four women who opened up to her over six years."

—Nilanjana Roy, *The Financial Times*

The Newlyweds

The
Newlyweds

Rearranging Marriage in Modern India

Mansi Choksi

ATRIA PAPERBACK

New York   London   Toronto   Sydney   New Delhi

ATRIA
PAPERBACK

An Imprint of Simon & Schuster, LLC
1230 Avenue of the Americas
New York, NY 10020

Some dialogue has been re-created.

First Atria Paperback edition June 2024

ATRIA PAPERBACK and colophon are trademarks of Simon & Schuster, LLC

Simon & Schuster: Celebrating 100 Years of Publishing in 2024

For information about special discounts for bulk purchases, please contact Simon & Schuster Special Sales at 1-866-506-1949 or business@simonandschuster.com.

The Simon & Schuster Speakers Bureau can bring authors to your live event. For more information or to book an event, contact the Simon & Schuster Speakers Bureau at 1-866-248-3049 or visit our website at www.simonspeakers.com.

Interior design by Dana Sloan

Manufactured in the United States of America

1 3 5 7 9 10 8 6 4 2

Library of Congress Cataloging-in-Publication Data
Names: Choksi, Mansi, author.
Title: The newlyweds : rearranging marriage in modern India / by Mansi Choksi.
Description: First Atria Books hardcover edition. | New York : Atria Books, 2022.
Identifiers: LCCN 2021049559 | ISBN 9781982134440 (hardcover) | ISBN 9781982134457 (paperback) | ISBN 9781982134464 (ebook)
Subjects: LCSH: Marriage—India—History—21st century. | Love—India—History—21st century. | Couples—India—History—21st century. | Elopement—India—History—21st century.
Classification: LCC HQ670.C45 2022 | DDC 306.810954—dc23/eng/20211014
LC record available at https://lccn.loc.gov/2021049559

ISBN 978-1-9821-3444-0
ISBN 978-1-9821-3445-7 (pbk)
ISBN 978-1-9821-3446-4 (ebook)

For Suhail and Kabir

CONTENTS

Cast of Characters

NEETU AND DAWINDER

Neetu Rani, the daughter of a landlord from the village of Kakheri in the northern Indian state of Haryana. She is twenty-one, trim and stylish, with the ability to talk about the lives of Bollywood actors as if they are next of kin. She is a Hindu of the Panchal caste, a rank of goldsmiths, stonemasons, and carpenters, and is expected to stay home until she can be transferred to a husband through an arranged marriage.

Dawinder Singh, a twenty-four-year-old neighbor of Neetu Rani and the son of a retired truck driver. He is a Sikh of the Mehra caste of palanquin bearers and boatsmen that is considered marginally lower in the complex web of caste structure. He has a soft, cheerful face, a headful of curls, and a nervous laugh.

Gulzar Singh, also known as Kala, Neetu's father. He is the short-tempered owner of a firewood shop and a landlord. With two successful businesses, a two-bedroom house, and a son in the Indian Navy, he is considered an influential man in the village.

Sudesh Rani, Neetu's mother and Kala's wife. She quietly protects her daughters from her husband's temper in a place where women are expected to fade into the background in the presence of men.

Gurmej Singh, Dawinder's father, a sickly man who drove trucks for a living until his eyesight grew weak. He dreams of growing old in his ancestral fields in the village of his birth.

Sukhwinder Kaur, Dawinder's mother, a god-fearing woman and devoted wife.

Kulwant Kaur, Dawinder's aunt, who lives in a neighboring province. She is a wealthy veterinarian's wife with jet-black hair and loose wrinkled skin who prides herself on taming feral daughters-in-law.

Sanjoy Sachdev, chairman of the Love Commandos, a vigilante group that protects couples marked for honor killings by their families. He likes to be addressed as Baba (Grandfather), even though he is "only eighteen with thirty-eight years of experience."

Manoj and Babli, young lovers from a village near Kakheri, who are murdered for bringing dishonor to their families by defying the caste system and marrying each other.

MONIKA AND ARIF

Monika Ingle, the youngest daughter of a Hindu trader of double cotton mattresses in the western city of Nagpur. She is eighteen, small, and delicate, with luminous skin and a glossy side braid.

Mohammad Arif Dosani, called Arif, the son of a Muslim shopkeeper in the village of Basmath who dreams of becoming a policeman. He is twenty-three, with pockmarked cheeks, a circular nod, and a heart he keeps ice cold while flirting with city girls.

Bhagyashri Ingle, called Bhaga, Monika's older sister. She is bold and outspoken. She meets Arif at a training for police constable recruits, and they become fast friends.

Shridhar Ingle, Monika and Bhagyashri's father. He is a trader of mattresses and the head of the Ingle household.

Ranjana Ingle, Monika and Bhagyashri's mother. She is a mild-mannered housewife.

Bashir Dosani, Arif's father. He is a small-boned man with a poetic bent who owns a children's clothes shop near a mosque in the village of Basmath.

Tabssum Dosani, Arif's mother, a bossy woman who likes to deliver her insults in a voice dripping with honey and who appoints herself in charge of the household and the business.

Akida Khemani, Arif's aunt, who also lives in Nagpur, with her own family. She loves Arif as much as her own children.

Vishal Punj, also known as Bajrangi Paji Saheb, the chief convener of the Bajrang Dal's Nagpur Metropolitan chapter, a belligerent Hindu nationalist youth group.

Madhav Sadashiv Golwalkar (1906–73), a zoology professor from a village near Nagpur, who took over the reins of the Rashtriya Swayamsevak Sangh, a Far Right quasi-militant group devoted to the creation of a Hindu nation.

RESHMA AND PREETHI

Reshma Mokenwar, a twenty-eight-year-old sales assistant from a Mumbai suburb. She has a heart-shaped face stained yellow from a lifetime of turmeric fairness treatments and a tongue sharpened through the knife grinder of a bad marriage.

Preethi Sarikela, an eighteen-year-old daughter of Reshma's father's cousin sister from the village of Bazarhathnoor in the southern state of Telangana.

Babu Mokenwar, Reshma's father, who works as a driver in the city of Mumbai.

Rekha Mokenwar, Reshma's mother, who earns a living by scrubbing dirty dishes.

Kishen Mokenwar, the younger of Reshma's two brothers, who is named after the Hindu god of love and dreams of becoming a local politician.

Narsa Sarikela, Preethi's mother and Reshma's aunt, a farmhand whose small frame is hunched over from a lifetime of picking cotton in the fields of Bazarhathnoor.

Ushanna Sarikela, Preethi's father, a worker in the village's irrigation department.

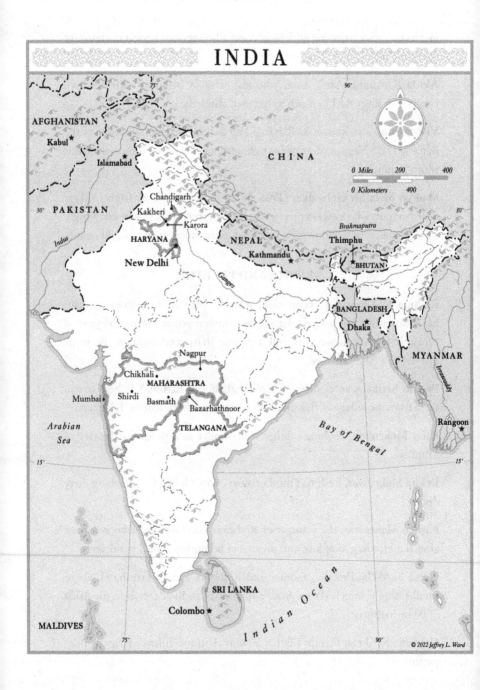

INDIA

AFGHANISTAN
Kabul ★

Islamabad ★

CHINA

PAKISTAN

0 Miles   200   400

0 Kilometers   400

30°   30°

Indus

Chandigarh
Kakheri
Karora

HARYANA

New Delhi

Ganges

NEPAL
Kathmandu ★

Brahmaputra

Thimphu
★
BHUTAN

BANGLADESH
Dhaka ★

MYANMAR

Irrawaddy

Nagpur

Chikhali
MAHARASHTRA

Mumbai •   Shirdi
Basmath
Bazarhathnoor
TELANGANA

Arabian
Sea

Bay of Bengal

Rangoon
★

15°   15°

SRI LANKA

Colombo ★

Indian Ocean

MALDIVES

75°   90°

© 2022 Jeffrey L. Ward

Introduction

F or most of my mother's life, she has lived in the house she was born in. It is a roomy apartment on the second floor of a building with curving, dark stairs in an old part of Mumbai. Every afternoon, the sunlight presses through the stained glass windows of the corridor. Its big bedroom windows open into the canopies of trees. There is a powder-blue wall populated with old photographs of the city, and the drawers still sometimes reveal the belongings of people who spent part of their lives in this house, then moved on to go somewhere else. They include my great-grandparents, grandparents, uncles and aunts, cousins, my sister, and me.

When my mother was eighteen, she fell in love with a man and married him against her family's wishes. After her eleven-year-long marriage crumbled, she returned to the house with two daughters. Even though she has lived in the same place for forty-eight years since, she carries an air of displacement everywhere she goes. She is always in a hurry. In a hurry to get somewhere. In a hurry to return. In a hurry to leave again. But to go where?

When I met the young couples whose stories make up this book, they were consumed with that same hurry. I met Neetu and Dawinder days after they had run away from their village and landed in the grip of a journalist-activist who promised to protect them. Weeks later, I met Monika and Arif when they were on the run from right-wing vigilantes. Finally, when I met Reshma and Preethi, a lesbian couple struggling to start their lives together in a town where they knew no one, I came to realize that the pursuit of love and its aftermath was ultimately a kind of displacement.

◆┈┈◇┈┈▶

Two in every three Indians is under the age of thirty-five. No other country has more young people. Yet we are torn about whether it is acceptable to be young and do the things young people do. If a survey asked us who we were or where we were going, we were expected to say that we are different from our parents because we look to the future and not to the past. Recently, such a survey was conducted, and it revealed that half our young people consider caste and religion to be the defining aspects of our identity. One-third of us believe that intercaste marriages will destroy Indian society. Half of us are completely opposed to interreligious marriage. Only one in seven of us approves of dating before marriage. Four in five of us married with permission from our parents, and less than 6 percent of us chose our own partners. Most of us think like our parents and conduct our lives based on the fear of disappointing them.

Marriage has a special place in Indian society. In many ways, it is the only intended outcome of growing up. It is an arrangement between two families belonging to the same warp and weft in the tapestry of religion, caste, class, clan, region, and language. The goal of marriage is to cement those boundaries to ensure the survival of power hierarchies because we are a society that places greater emphasis on collectivism than individualism. We derive our identities from the groups we belong to; our daily lives and our politics are arranged around them. When young people choose their own partners, we threaten order with chaos.

I wanted to know if love can endure with dignity if it becomes tainted with shame. I learned there is a great power in longing for love, but once we attain that love at the cost of moral injury, that space can become filled with a longing for acceptance.

◆┄┄◇┄┄▶

Often when love is gained, it can start to feel unheroic. The process of reconciliation with our choices can be both beautiful and terrible. There is an expectation in Indian society that even if married life turns out to be hell, women will stay in the marriage and pray for the same partner for the next seven lifetimes. Our bodies are repositories of family honor, battlefields for political wars, and instruments for reproduction.

While reporting on the lives of these three couples, I often thought about why Indian society does not implode from the pressures of so many young people—especially young women—pushing against what we want and what we are expected to want. It also made me think about whether curiosity was really a trait that could be gained and then given up.

Neetu and Dawinder, Arif and Monika, and Reshma and Preethi grew up in villages and towns in different corners of the country, each of them internalizing a narrow spectrum of morality and an overwhelming sense of duty. They are exactly the kind of young Indians who are raised to resist the urge to surpass the boundaries of traditional Indian society. So, after they risk everything for the sake of love, they suddenly cannot recognize themselves. Each of them is tormented by one central question: Was it worth it?

Late one evening, when I went back to my mother's home after spending the day reporting, I asked her if her decision to marry the man she fell in love with all those years earlier had been worth it. "I don't know," she answered.

We took our dinner plates to the television and sat down to watch a Hindi soap opera about another doomed romance.

PART ONE

Chapter 1

Kakheri

On the night of November 27, 2016, Dawinder Singh dropped off a bottle of sleeping pills outside his neighbor's door. Everyone in Kakheri, his village in the northern Indian state of Haryana, believed him to be gone, perhaps abroad. But here he was, a handkerchief tied over his mouth like a bandit, fleeing toward the bus stand. He was twenty-four, with a soft, cheerful face, a headful of curls, and a tendency to laugh at the wrong times. Inside the neighbor's house, Neetu Rani, the birdlike beauty he grew up adoring, was more composed. She was twenty-one, trim and stylish, with the ability to talk about the lives of Bollywood actors as though they were next of kin. She waited for her parents to finish their Hindi soap opera, and as soon as they went to bed, she went outside to pick up the pills.

Two nights later, Dawinder returned in a car with two cousins who had been persuaded to join his mission when they were already weak from watching romantic movies. One would drive the get-away car, and the other would provide moral support. The cousins watched music videos on their cell phones while they waited on the abandoned road that took freight trucks to marble factories nearby. Dawinder muttered prayers—the only way he knew to cope with uncertainties such as exam results, visa applications, and the out-come of eloping with a neighbor.

Inside, Neetu watched her parents finish bowls of rice and beans laced with the sleeping pills. After midnight, Dawinder's phone fi-nally rang. Neetu was scolding Dawinder in whispers: What kind of sleeping pills were these? Her parents had finished their dinner, but they were still shuffling around. Her father kept waking to go to the bathroom. Dawinder asked her to be patient and began pray-ing aloud.

An hour later, she called again, reporting that she had shaken her mother, pretending to be scared of the dark, but there was no response. Dawinder got out of the car and hurried to her house to help her haul out four suitcases containing twenty-three tunics, salwar suits, jeans and tops, old family albums, friendship bands, birthday cards, stuffed animals, and a life-size poster of herself that she'd had taken in a professional photo studio. She knew he would come barefoot, despite her having told him not to, so she had cleared away the fallen branches and razor-rimmed leaves from the babul tree. After the last suitcase, she scaled the wall herself, and they ran out laughing through the narrow dirt lane where they had first seen each other. A sharp right, and past the cowshed where she would hide to take his phone calls. Another right, and past their school. On the corner, her father's firewood shop. Finally, into the car.

The vehicle was moving, but it was hard to see where it was going in the thick blanket of smog that descended across northern India in the winter. In the back seat, Dawinder slipped a set of twenty-one bangles around Neetu's wrists: reds and golds stacked between whites and silvers. This was her *choora*, the marker of a new bride. If she wore it for a year, Dawinder would be guaranteed a long life. He tied a *mangalsutra*, a thread of small black beads that looked like a sprinkling of black mustard seeds, around her neck and painted the part in her hair with vermilion powder that he carried in the fold of an old newspaper sheet. Neetu was now his wife, he announced. She thought that their love story was just like in the movies, only without nice costumes.

As the car sped onto the highway, Neetu felt herself floating. Outside the window, rice fields flew past. Suddenly she felt her stomach churning, and she realized she needed to vomit. The car screeched to a halt, and she climbed out to throw up. A few miles ahead, she needed to stop again. And then again.

Three hours and five episodes of retching later, the cousins dropped Neetu and Dawinder at a bus stop in Rajpura, a town forty miles from home. When the bus came, they found seats by the window. Neetu rested her head on Dawinder's shoulder and described the agony of waiting for her parents to drift off to sleep. "Who knows when they will be able to eat or rest again," she said.

The sun was rising when the bus rolled through a traffic jam outside New Delhi. Dawinder saw a big, heaving city packed with crowds that could swallow them up and provide the anonymity they needed to survive. Neetu's eyes watered from the pollution.

Dawinder called his aunt Kulwant Kaur, who he suspected would be his only relative able to receive the news of his elopement without collapsing. She asked to speak to his new bride. "Don't betray him now," Kulwant said. Neetu promised that she would not.

They hailed a rickshaw, which bobbed in and out of potholes and squirmed through waves of pedestrians. Neetu saw a storefront that displayed red, blue, and yellow bras. In her village, she had been able to buy them only in white. They rode past cheap hotels that offered rooms by the hour, places where married men took their mistresses. Dawinder clutched her hand and told her to trust him.

The rickshaw stopped outside a rusted gate. They looked up at a crumbling building covered in lime plaster, scaffolding, and saris hung to dry. Outside, men were smoking and staring. Dawinder had seen videos of this place online, but in person it looked nothing like he had expected. It was too late to turn back now—they had saved up ten thousand rupees (about $150) to reserve a space. He took out his cell phone.

"Hello, Love Commandos," the voice on the line said.

"We have come," Dawinder said.

"We have been waiting for you."

◆┄┄◇┄┄➤

In Kakheri, the news of Neetu's and Dawinder's disappearance broke with sunrise. Neetu's father, Gulzar Singh, a landlord known as Kala, walked around the bazaar looking crazed. With his wrestler's physique and a pencil-thin mustache, Kala resembled the villain from a 1980s television adaptation of the *Mahabharata*, the Hindu epic in which each character is meant to embody a trait that is supremely good or evil.

Neetu's mother, Sudesh Rani, sat in her kitchen sobbing as neighbors gathered to commiserate, for a runaway daughter was as good as dead. Women in rural Haryana are required to cover their heads, fade into the background in the presence of men, and make informed guesses about what their husbands would like to eat for dinner. Young girls are expected to stay home until they can be transferred to a husband through an arranged marriage. Neetu had disgraced her family not only by eloping but also by doing so with the short, slow-witted son of a neighbor.

According to rural custom, men and women of the same village are considered to be siblings, which put Neetu and Dawinder's relationship under the umbrella of incest. Worse, Dawinder was a Sikh, from the Mehra caste of palanquin bearers and boatsmen. His father, Gurmej Singh, who had driven a truck for a pittance for most of his life, turned to farming when his eyesight grew weak. Neetu was a Hindu of the Panchal caste, a rank of goldsmiths, stonemasons, and carpenters. Her father, with his own firewood shop and a son in the navy, was a respectable man in the community.

In rural Haryana, when romantic relationships become ensnared by taboos, the consequences were often fatal. In 2007 the bodies of Manoj and Babli Banwala, lovers from the same village, were found in gunnysacks that had been dumped in a canal not far from Kakheri. After kidnapping the couple, Babli's family forced her to drink pesticide and strangled Manoj to death in front of her. With support from leaders in their village, Babli's relatives saw the murders as the only punishment commensurate with their humiliation.

Neetu and Dawinder's match should have been unthinkable. When they met in 2005, her family had just moved up the street. She was nine, and he was twelve. After school, Dawinder would play video games with Neetu's brother, Deepak, and Neetu and her sister, Ruksana, would play house with Dawinder's sister, Jasbir. The families got along well for a few years, until one afternoon in 2009, when Deepak grabbed Dawinder's neck during an argument. Neetu's father, Kala, who was known to have a short fuse, broke them up and slapped Dawinder across the face. After the incident, the families stopped talking. Besides, the children were entering their teens, and it was not proper for young girls and boys to be seen together.

The village practiced a separation of the sexes. Neetu's parents, for instance, observed a version of *sannyasa*, the Hindu philosophy of renunciation, which in retirement forbids physical contact with the opposite sex. If Neetu's father sat down on the rope cot, her mother would jump up as though something had bitten her.

In the summer of 2010, a year after the families cut ties, Dawinder noticed Neetu looking at him on the walk home from school. When he got to his house, he made himself a cup of tea and climbed onto a stool in his parents' room, curious whether he could see his neighbor from the window. She was out on her terrace, still watching him from a distance. Seeing that no one else was around, he raised his glass to her. Neetu responded by bursting into laughter. She was fourteen, and he was seventeen.

Dawinder was sure that this girl was trying to get him into trouble. But every day after that, Neetu would dawdle on the way home so that the two of them could talk. If they were alone at home, they would run into each other's houses and whisper sweet nothings: "That shirt looks good on you," she would say; "You look pretty with your hair loose," he would reply.

Neetu could not bear to think of herself as "that type of girl," which was the type of girl with a boyfriend, so she gave up meat for sixteen Mondays to convince Lord Shiva, a supreme Hindu deity, to turn Dawinder into her husband. On Karwa Chauth, the Hindu festival in which married women fast until moonrise for the safety of their husbands, Neetu secretly went hungry all day. When the wives of the village gathered on their roofs in shimmering bridal saris to break their fasts, Neetu watched them wistfully from her window. As the women glimpsed the moon and their husbands through the net of kitchen sieves, Neetu held up a tea strainer in the direction of Dawinder's window. "All I pray is that Lord Shiva accepts my fast and makes us husband and wife," she said to a thumb-sized photo of Dawinder.

Within two years, in March 2012, their relationship was discovered. One night after dinner, assuming her parents were asleep, Neetu snuck into Dawinder's house. The two had hardly a moment together before her mother started banging at the main door. Neetu panicked and slid under his bed but her mother pulled her out and started beating her, slapping her face and shoulders.

"Why did you come here?" Sudesh Rani hit her daughter until a cut opened above her lip. "Did he touch you anywhere?"

"We were just talking," Neetu cried.

"You jumped into his bed to talk?" she scoffed. "Should I wake your father and tell him where I found you in the middle of the night?"

Sudesh Rani dragged Neetu out by her hair. At the door, she warned Dawinder that if he wanted to live, he should disappear before she felt compelled to tell her husband.

For most of her life, Neetu had felt her mother's love drain all her worries, like a scalp massage after a long day out in the sun. When she was three, and a mysterious illness turned her legs into jelly, her mother walked barefoot from temple to temple, offering up her gold earrings and bangles to various gods and goddesses and giving up one favorite food after another to persuade them to cure her daughter. After the miracle really happened the year Neetu turned four, Sudesh Rani vowed to protect her daughter from her husband's temper. She promised to buy her a roti machine so that Neetu would not have to risk blistering her precious hands feeding kindling into a clay oven to make bread after marriage. But the day after Sudesh Rani found Neetu hiding under Dawinder's bed, she sent the girl away to her own mother's house in the nearby town of Jind as a final gesture of her affection. Weeks later, Neetu was sent to a strict all-girls boarding school, where, in order to scrub out temptations of youth, young women were forbidden from using phones, applying makeup, or wearing jeans.

In the house across the street, Dawinder's parents prepared to sell a chunk of their ancestral land. After hearing about Sudesh Rani's threat against their son, they decided that now was as good a time as any to send Dawinder to England to study business management, in the hope of eventually immigrating.

Even though their family had lived honorably in Kakheri for three generations since Dawinder's grandfather bought up tracts of barren land during the partition of Punjab in 1947 into Hindu-majority India and Muslim-majority Pakistan and tilled them until they turned green, they were prepared to sell everything to send their son to safety.

"Mummyji, what color is this shirt?" Dawinder pulled out a red shirt from the trunk as he gathered his clothes.

"Betaji, it is tomato red," his mother answered absentmindedly.

"No," he said. "It is blood red."

Sukhwinder Kaur burst into tears. Her son's habit of loading mundanities with deep meaning ever since he had become involved with the neighbor's girl suddenly filled her with contempt for his choices.

◆┄┄◇┄┄▶

Late one night, three months after Dawinder left for London, Neetu had a nightmare about him. They were running up the stairs of a dilapidated building, away from an angry mob wielding swords and axes, until they made it to a roof that was falling off in slabs. There was a pot of gold coins within their reach, but instead of grabbing it, they declared that they wished to get married. Suddenly the floor beneath their feet crashed, and, as Neetu saw herself fall, a quickening in her stomach woke her up. For weeks after that, she worried that something bad had happened to Dawinder. She kept trying to get in touch with him, but after a while the calls stopped going through.

In London, Dawinder had discovered that the university he was to study at was a sham that existed only on paper. The Indian owners had closed up shop and run away with his family's life savings. He went hungry for days until he was taken in by a Sikh family who allowed him to work as a stock boy at their supermarket without valid papers. They gave him warm clothes, food, and a place to sleep.

Dawinder and Neetu, who was still at boarding school, managed to get back in touch. She begged her classmates to let her receive his calls on cell phones they kept hidden behind toilet tanks. The two would discuss who ate what for lunch, gossip about her brother's love affairs, and assess the profound obstacles facing their relationship. He would tease her about how her eyes grew wide and her face turned into her father's when she became angry. She would respond by sending goofy selfies.

Dawinder's boss would ask him, "Betaji, why don't you get married to a nice British girl and settle down here?" "No, Uncleji," he would answer. "Someone is waiting for me in my village."

Two years later, in 2014, when Dawinder was arrested for transporting unlicensed liquor and deported back to India for working without valid papers, he was partly relieved. He was miserable without Neetu, as if an organ had been ripped out of his body.

Since it was too dangerous for Dawinder to return to Kakheri, the young man shuttled between the homes of two aunts and an uncle that were scattered across the northern Indian countryside. Everywhere he went, he was unable to sleep, stirred awake easily by the washing of pots and pans, locks and latches turning, and the distant mewls of stray cats.

Late one night, after being woken by the TV outside his room, Dawinder tried to put himself back to bed by imagining what Neetu looked like asleep, but the thoughts made his heart ache even more. When he wandered into his cousin Shanty's room, rubbing and shielding his eyes from the glow of the TV, he saw his cousin hypnotized by the movie actor Aamir Khan.

"There is no force over love; it is the triumphant fire, Ghalib. It cannot be stamped out, nor can it burn once doused," the actor's voice boomed as he recited an Urdu couplet by the nineteenth-century poet Mirza Asadullah Baig Khan on his popular television talk show, *Satyamev Jayate*. This episode of the program, which exposed grim social realities such as corruption, hunger, and unemployment in the hope of shaming millions of viewers out of their thick-skinned apathy, focused on the crisis of love marriages.

Dawinder's cousin was in a trance watching the famous actor weep as he told real stories of young lovers who were hunted by their own families for defying taboos regarding caste and religion. "We have young people whose hearts are burning with that fire of love, and we have parents of young people who are trying to douse that fire," Khan said. As he introduced a vigilante group that provided protection to young couples who wanted to marry for love, Dawinder let himself drop onto the sofa next to his cousin.

"Be strong, young lovers," Sanjoy Sachdev, the chairman of the Love Commandos, said to a thumping and whistling studio audience. Sachdev, an older man with an infant's face and large, green eyes, described his mission to help young lovers marry. His organization assisted them in navigating the red tape of getting weddings registered legally, offered free housing and food, and even risked its members' own lives to protect them. "There's an old song that always rings in my ears: 'We will love each other shamelessly, we will not fear the world,'" Sachdev told the audience. Dawinder stood up to clap in front of the television, his eyes brimming and his nostrils trembling with reverence.

Chapter 2

The Love Commandos

A little after nine, Neetu Rani and Dawinder Singh climbed up the dark, curving stairs of a crumbling four-story building across the street from a row of cheap hotels behind the New Delhi railway station, which may have been brothels. On the first landing, a dog named Romeo sniffed them for guns and explosives, and a rotating cast of young men led them into a three-bedroom apartment. Past a metal grille, a mini fridge, and a wall shrine of assorted Hindu deities, in a room cluttered with newspapers, ashtrays, and biscuits, an older man dressed in a matching tracksuit sat in a plastic lawn chair, conducting three different phone conversations at once.

"Why is the administration and police machinery criminally silent on implementing the standing directions of the honorable Supreme Court?" he said into one phone.

"Son, in fifteen minutes, the situation will settle down, and the police will release her," he muttered into another.

19

And into a third phone: "Yadavji, do me a favor and let this love couple pass your jurisdiction safely." He turned around to nod at Neetu and Dawinder and gestured at them to sit down on the edge of a tattered bed.

This was Sanjoy Sachdev, the cofounder and chairman of Love Commandos. He looked unwashed and reeked of cigarettes, but everything he uttered sounded like poetry to Neetu and Dawinder. He ordered tea and spiced rice flakes for breakfast, then told them that even the Hindu deities Shiva and Parvati married each other against caste tradition.

"The world's first intercaste marriage was between Lord Shiva and Mother Parvati," he said. "None of their families were happy. They did not accept it. So what did they do? They exchanged garlands in the mountains and became husband and wife. No one was ready to go along with them, so they arranged a wedding procession of ghosts. The enemies of love screaming in the name of religion today don't understand that what they are opposing is a path set out by Lord Shiva himself."

Dawinder nodded solemnly. Neetu looked over his shoulder to observe two women in the kitchen. They heaped spiced rice flakes onto small plates and poured tea into a tray of mismatched cups. She thought it was too bold for maids to laugh and let cups and saucers clink in full view of guests.

The Love Commandos operated like a family, Sachdev continued, so couples were required to call him Baba, meaning Grandfather, even though he was "only sweet eighteen with thirty-eight years of experience." He oversaw the couples' marriage registration process so that they could not be legally separated. The three other middle-aged Commandos, who lived in the neighboring building, were to be addressed as Papa. Each had an area of expertise. Harsh Malhotra, a former interior decorator and local politician, coordinated rescue operations of couples in distress. Sonu Rangi, a former worker for the Hindu nationalist Shiv Sena Party, organized weddings of runaway couples. Govinda Chand, a part-time graduate student, took care of groceries and bills.

"I am sure you want to know why us old mad men risk our lives for young people like you," he said. "Let me tell you a story. Once, a small boy asked an old man why he was planting a mango tree. 'Dada, by the time this tree bears fruit, you will probably be dead. Even if you are still alive, you won't have any teeth left to eat the fruit. So then why are you wasting your time?' The old man smiled at the boy and said, 'Son, I am not planting this mango tree for me. I'm planting it for your children. By the time this tree grows, you will have children just about as big as you, and it is them who will savor the sweet fruits of my efforts.'

"I am planting a mango tree called Love Commandos," Sachdev continued. "I am risking my life for you today so that your children can inherit a country where love is not a crime. It is my small effort for a new and bright India."

Before he showed Neetu and Dawinder their room, Sachdev explained the rules of the shelter: no sex, no afternoon naps, and no contact with the outside world. Everything was free, including shelter, food, and legal aid, but since they were a volunteer organization and they had already sold their cars, flats, and gold to protect runaway lovers, each couple was expected to pay for their own wedding. Neetu and Dawinder were so grateful that, without being asked, they handed over Dawinder's debit card and gave Baba the PIN.

◆┄┄◇┄┄➤

Their room was at the end of a dark corridor. With its low ceiling, blue-green walls, and gloomy views of a concrete roof, it felt as if the air had been deliberately sucked out. A thin fluorescent tube light flickered all day above a small television that streamed back-to-back episodes of a Hindi soap opera about a dutiful housewife who was really a mythical, shape-shifting cobra.

Neetu surveyed the room morosely as three other couples they were to share it with introduced themselves, including the two women she had seen in the kitchen and mistaken for domestic help. Sanjay, a rickshaw driver from the city of Ahmedabad in western India, was with Bhavika, a landowner's daughter from a higher caste. Prashant and Sheetal, college friends from the northern Indian town of Amroha, were on the run because they belonged to the same clan, and even though they were not directly related, their relationship was considered incest. Afsana, a Muslim housekeeper from East Delhi, was with Malkit, the Sikh heir to a readymade clothes shop in West Delhi. As the couples started to exchange notes about the varying amounts they had paid to reserve a place at the shelter, they heard a knock on the door.

"Children?" Sanjoy Sachdev's voice rang out. "Your wedding is in ten minutes."

As Neetu dabbed the pink of her lipstick on her cheeks, she wished she had brought a brocade salwar suit and gotten a chance to get her hair done at a beauty salon. Dawinder threw on a clean shirt and styled his hair into a disarray.

Sonu Rangi, who sported a handlebar mustache and an explosion of canned laughter for his mobile ring tone, led them past shops selling spare motorcycle parts, stalls stacked with pens and note-books, and carts displaying plastic flip phones. Dawinder hurried to keep up with Rangi, while Neetu got left behind in a knot of people milling at the shopping stands. When she turned a corner at a row of lawyers in flapping black coats perched on plastic stools to solicit clients, she was on the verge of tears.

"I'm here." Dawinder took her hand. "I'm right here." So much was changing so fast that it was hard to understand if she was crying because she had suddenly lost him or because she suddenly felt lost.

In an apartment on the top floor of a tin-roofed building that had been converted into a temple, Neetu and Dawinder sat cross-legged in front of a holy fire as a priest with sandalwood paste on his fore-head chanted Vedic scriptures. Sonu Rangi sat in a corner, talking into his cell phone and gesturing for the rituals to continue.

The couple circled the holy fire seven times and vowed to be to-gether for seven births, the entirety of time it is believed for a soul to break free from the cycle of births and deaths, according to Hindu philosophy. They signed a religious marriage certificate and posed for a photograph as evidence. Then the couple waited at the door with a box of sweets in their hands and listened to curses drift out of the stairwell as Rangi and the priest negotiated the payment.

When they arrived back at the shelter, jasmine and rose garlands still around their necks, the other couples stood in the doorway to receive them. "Mr. and Mrs. Dawinder Singh," Sachdev announced from his bed. "Where are my sweets?" The last step to legally for-malize their wedding was to submit the religious certificate to the government marriage registrar. Sachdev would take care of that.

◆┄┄◇┄┄◆

Before starting the Love Commandos, Sachdev had tried to open a poultry farm, a sweetened-milk company, and a factory for car parts. All three businesses tanked. He worked briefly as a consultant to Indian Railways, entered and lost a local election, and finally became a journalist. But he sensed that he was meant for a larger purpose. One Valentine's Day in the early 2000s, a colleague in the newsroom told him about the Hindu nationalist groups that roamed parks and college campuses to protest the Western corruption of Indian values. They beat up couples, cut their hair, sprayed them with chili powder, and pronounced them brother and sister. Hearing of the victims suffering for their love, Sachdev thought, *Who are these people to poke their dirty nose in between?*

In 2010, when honor killings started to dominate television news debates, he got the idea to create Love Commandos. Sachdev didn't like the word *runaways*, so he referred to his clients as "people leaving parental homes for the unification of the love family." He wanted them to relish their freedom. "This country is sitting on a volcano," he said. "This is a country of six hundred and fifty million young people. Each young person has a heart that is burning with a flame called love."

Through local newspaper reporting, the Love Commandos were made aware of at least four bounties that were issued by *khap panchayats* for protecting runaway couples. Khap panchayats, unelected councils of upper-caste elders in the countryside, routinely issued diktats for disturbing the delicate balance of the caste system. They did not have any government-sanctioned authority, but they wielded extraordinary influence over their communities. Once, while the daughter of a local politician was taking shelter with the group, a mob burst in and took turns beating and kicking the Commandos. But within a week, they were back on their feet, helping a new runaway couple get married.

As it turned out, Sachdev had never been in love himself—it was only his work. "I didn't have time to fall in love," he said, "because I was busy solving other people's problems." At twenty-eight, he entered an arranged marriage. His wife lived in his hometown, thirty miles from New Delhi, and took care of his aging father. Sometimes Sachdev would go to see her, but months might pass between visits, since planning trips depended on his mood. They had four children, now grown, who had given him what he described as "an eternal feeling of love."

◆┄┄◇┄┄➤

As Neetu and Dawinder clicked photographs on the shelter's balcony soon after their wedding in New Delhi, Dawinder's father, Gurmej Singh, took his brother-in-law to a hospital in Ladwa, a town a hundred miles away. While there, Gurmej silenced three calls. Two were from his younger brother, and one was from the village chief. When his phone rang a fourth time, he started to worry. His wife, Sukhwinder Kaur, was away on a pilgrimage in a distant village, and Dawinder was supposed to have started work at a relative's shop in a neighboring province. "Only God can save us," Gurmej's younger brother sobbed on the phone and asked him to meet outside the hospital gate. "Only God can save us now."

When Gurmej reached the hospital gate, the side door of a van slid open. Neetu's uncle and cousins pulled Gurmej inside and wedged him into the middle seat. His younger brother, who was in the back seat, stared back in guilty silence.

"What happened?" Gurmej said in a heavy voice as the van jerked to a start. "What are you doing?"

"Where did he take her?" Neetu's father, Kala, turned in the front seat to look Gurmej in the eye.

By the time Gurmej figured out that his son had run away with a neighbor's girl from the village, the van was speeding down an empty highway. The men in the car deliberated whether it would be more satisfying to slash Gurmej's neck and dump his dead body in a gutter or drag him to the police station and force him to reveal the couple's whereabouts. The village chief, who was crouched in the back seat, advised against the first idea, since wriggling out of murder charges had been getting trickier lately, even if wads of cash were dangled in the faces of salivating policemen.

Three hours later, the men sat across from Jitender Kumar, the inspector in charge at the Siwan Police Station, who was stretched out on a mattress in a khaki uniform unbuttoned to his waist. He sent for plastic chairs from a marriage hall nearby and ordered a round of tea and biscuits. Kala asked the police officer to compel Gurmej Singh to reveal where the couple was hiding. Neetu's uncle shoved Gurmej toward the inspector. "We have lost our daughter, our honor, our everything," he spat. "Because of this bastard's son."

The inspector took a long sip of tea and explained he had already been informed about Neetu and Dawinder by the Love Commandos, who were protecting the couple at their safe house in New Delhi. Unfortunately, he said, there was no law that could stop two adults from marrying who they wanted.

◆◦◦◦◆

In New Delhi, as the sun slanted through the shelter's balcony, Sanjoy Sachdev burst into a song about a boy who slept through life and woke only when he had turned into an old man. "Awake, oh traveler, for dawn has come. The night is no more that you sleep." His face softened as he sang. "He who sleeps will lose. He who wakes will gain."

When he could no longer recall the lyrics, Sachdev opened his eyes and sat up in bed. Dawinder was sweeping the floor of his room, and Neetu was dusting the shelves.

"Understood?" Sachdev asked them in his singsong voice.

"Yes, Baba," Neetu answered with a grin as clouds of dust rose in the air. "You are telling us to wake up early and fill up water in buckets and tumblers before the municipality turns off the supply."

"This is the meaning you got from these beautiful words?" Sachdev snorted. "And you call yourselves a love couple?"

"I'll tell you," Dawinder said. "There is no time for sleep because there is so much left to do for the sake of our mummy-daddy."

"Sit down." Baba slapped his thigh. "This is the tragedy of India's love couples." Sachdev usually started these kinds of conversations after he had downed a few quarters of rum or when he was in the company of a prospective donor. He would launch into impassioned speeches about the fundamental rights to life and liberty, the scourge of capitalism, and the nostalgia of old-school romance. He would start breathing heavily, abruptly go silent, then sigh and suddenly remember an Urdu couplet.

Dawinder sat on the foot of his bed to listen while Neetu continued tidying the room. Sachdev explained why he wanted them to know the stories of two couples: Hakim-Mehwish and Pratibha-Devasheesh. Their lives were lessons that belonged to every young person living in India in the twenty-first century, he said gravely. It was important for every young person, including Neetu and Dawinder—especially Neetu and Dawinder—to know the mistakes they had made.

Hakim Abdul and Mehwish, a couple from a village in the Bulandshahr district, were on the run when they sought sanctuary with the Love Commandos. Sachdev said Mehwish gave birth to a daughter while they were at the shelter, and Hakim interviewed for bank jobs with the organization's help. But one day, Hakim snuck out of the shelter to visit his sick mother despite the Commandos' warning that it was still dangerous. Days later, he was shot dead on the outskirts of his village, allegedly by members of Mehwish's family.

Pratibha Gurjar and Devasheesh Meena, lovers from different castes, were on their way to the shelter when their families claimed to have a change of heart. Pratibha's father invited her back home to attend her sister's wedding and promised to send her to Devasheesh after the festivities were over. Days later, when he called to talk to Pratibha, her father informed him that she had died in a freak accident.

"Did anything go inside your thick heads?" Sachdev said. "Their mistake was that they fell into the trap of going back to their parents."

As he went on to explain the importance of a three-year cooling-off period before couples reinitiated contact with their families, the blood drained from Dawinder's face.

Over the next days, Neetu had a recurring nightmare. She saw Dawinder running toward her with his arms outstretched. She waited for him to sweep her up in his arms and envelop her in his love, but he fell into water and disappeared. Even though they were finally together, Neetu found herself vanishing into flares of fear that they would be ripped apart, especially after hearing the morbid endings of so many love stories that had passed through the shelter.

"Stop thinking so much," Dawinder told his bride when she cried. "God will show us the right path."

Taking his advice, to focus on positive thoughts, Neetu started to keep a diary of the moments that brought her joy: the first time she and Dawinder kissed, the morning they showered together, the night they spoke on the phone for almost eight hours.

"Remember how we used to talk from night to morning?" she said to him as she wrote in her diary. "Even if I had to go to the bathroom, I would take the phone with me so the line would not get cut."

Sachdev was sitting nearby, drinking a glass of water and trying to keep a straight face, but he started laughing so hard that he spat out of his mouth.

"What did you talk about for so long?" he wanted to know.

"I keep telling her, Baba, 'How much will you talk?'" Dawinder said. His face crumpled with embarrassment. "I saved so much money in England, but all of it went in phone bills when I came back home."

"But, Baba, why didn't he have the brains to buy a mega bundle of talk time?" Neetu said. "Everyone knows that turns out to be cheaper in the long run."

Sachdev suddenly went off. "Have you studied economics?" he thundered. "What is credibility? Credit is how much money you can borrow. That is your credit. Here is cash, there is cash. In India, there is no credit on any human being. Credibility is over!"

Dawinder nodded like a bobblehead doll. He knew that the older man's random outbursts were usually triggered by hunger. "If I had to talk to someone for thirty minutes, I would go mad," Sachdev went on. "After two hours, I would walk myself into a coffin and sit inside it."

"Baba," Dawinder said as he covered Sachdev's feet with a blanket, "let me make you a nice cup of tea."

Chapter 3

Snakes and Mongooses

The first time Monika Ingle sat on the back of Mohammad Arif Dosani's motorbike one summer afternoon in 2015, he slammed on the front brakes to make her tumble toward him in the hope of sparking a romance. Arif, as he was called, was a villager from the drought belt in the western Indian state of Maharashtra. He was twenty-three, with pockmarked cheeks, a circular nod, and a heart he kept ice cold while flirting with city girls.

In the short distance to a suburban district with gorgeous views of the Kanhan River, where the rest of their friends were waiting, Arif intentionally hit the brakes twice. Monika still sat straight as a pole, as if she were welded to the seat. She was eighteen, small and delicate, with luminous skin, a glossy side braid, and a perpetually stunned expression, her large eyes flicked on like headlights. At a traffic signal, when Arif turned around to give his passenger an impish smile, she scowled and told him to keep his eyes on the road.

For the rest of his years, whenever Arif entered one of his meditative moods, searching for the turning point of his life, he returned to this memory. In every telling, it took a different form. It was this moment that filled his world with colors. It was this moment that sentenced him to a life of destructive sorrow.

◆┄┄◇┄┄➤

In 1992, when Arif was a newborn in Basmath, a village in the far corner of western India, communal riots ripped through the country like a cyclone. A mob of Hindu supremacists hoisting hammers and axes surged through the ancient byways of Ayodhya, a northern Indian town, and tore down the Babri Masjid, a sixteenth-century Mughal-era mosque. The demolition, the inflection point of a century-long campaign by the Hindu Right to reclaim the site as the birthplace of its deity Lord Ram, ignited one of the worst Hindu-Muslim riots since partition, the bloodbath that severed Pakistan from India in 1947.

After the mosque fell, Indian cities and towns braced for violence. Arif's family chanted prayers inside a dark room in their home in the Muslim stronghold of Khajipura. It was a ritual that had become second nature whenever Hindu-Muslim resentments boiled to the surface. When the fog of the riots lifted, thousands of people were dead, but Arif's family found themselves unharmed, with both their home and their shop still standing. For them, the events confirmed that Arif's birth had reinstated the family back into the cosmic wheel of good fortune.

The Dosani family had once been among the village's wealthiest. Arif's grandfather, a flamboyant man with business interests in horticulture, oils, and textiles, hosted grand feasts, performed charity work, and commanded the respect of multiple religious communities, including Sunni and Shiite Muslims, Jains, Buddhists, and Hindus.

However, after his sudden death, the family's star fell. Arif's father, Bashir, the youngest son of his fifth wife, was a small-boned man with a poetic bent of mind who struggled to save his share of the family businesses. By the time Arif was born, all that remained was a children's clothes shop, a room with flaking blue walls attached to the village mosque, where Bashir languished in a nest of frocks and dungarees. Arif's mother, Tabssum, a bossy woman who liked to deliver her insults in a honey-dipped voice, appointed herself in charge of the business. She would place baby Arif near the cash box, so that his luck would rub off where it mattered, and stand around importantly, one hip out, supervising her husband.

As a boy, Arif would linger after school with his best friend, Khaled, to see if they could join a cricket game, even though the other boys treated them with friendly condescension. Tabssum would stomp onto the cricket field to drag Arif home by one ear. "Do you enjoy getting fed insults? Do they taste sweet?" she would sing. Khaled, who had lost his left leg to polio, would totter behind the mother and son, using a bamboo stick as a crutch.

On the cricket field, his forehead glistening with sweat, Arif was at peace. But in the presence of textbooks, he felt himself shrivel up; alphabets and numbers scattered like red ants and crawled under his skin to drink his blood. When Arif failed the tenth grade, Tabssum yanked him by his hair and struck his legs with a broom as he bobbed and weaved around the room to dodge her blows.

But three years later, when he failed the twelfth grade, and Tabssum sat down to cry, Arif felt a cold stab of fear. Months earlier, his dreams of a cricket career had been doused by the sobering reality of his poverty. Despite being selected to play in a prestigious community tournament, beating out a hundred boys in the district, he watched his dream slip away because he could not gather enough money for a train ticket to the game. Without an exit plan, Arif came to realize, he would be stuck forever, withering away within the blue walls of the children's clothes shop.

Arif's desperation to leave the village before it became too late turned into a form of suffering. The longer he stayed in Basmath, the greater his chances of being swindled out of the glorious future predicted when he was born.

On his twentieth birthday, in the summer of 2012, Arif moved to Nagpur, a town two hundred miles east, to apprentice for his uncle Rehman Khemani, who managed a fleet of freight trucks. Hasanbagh, a Nagpur slum so hot that its roads melted in the summer, was the most miserable place Arif had ever set foot in. A criminal gang collected protection money from local businesses, drunks dragged their wives out of their homes by the hair, prostitutes solicited him, and stray goats ate his slippers. His uncle's stinking two-story shanty, where eight adults and one toddler studied, bathed, cried, cooked, fought, and slept, felt like it would burst into flame from the tempers sizzling inside.

At night, the torrential despair of the shanties dissipated into a vast darkness. When Arif returned home from work covered in the soot of engines, usually after Hasanbagh was lulled to sleep with the last television soap opera, he found his aunt Akida waiting up for him. Akida, a woman who kept her skeletal frame from buckling by strapping it together with a scarf, oiled his hair as they watched the moon swim up to their window.

Recently, Arif had seen a job listing for an office manager's post. Sitting inside a wooden booth at the corner hotel, poring over the newspaper with his tongue stuck out, he dreamed about returning triumphantly to his village with a white-collar job. But weeks passed, and he heard nothing on his job applications. "Your marks must be too low" was Akida's reading of the situation. Arif applied to more office jobs, and, as he watched boys with worse grades fill up the vacancies, his aunt's explanation started to feel inadequate. "They must have seen your name and thrown out your form," she tried again. This time it made perfect sense.

◆┄┄◇┄┄➤

The Indian constitution, the greatest document ever written, in Arif's opinion, for its emphasis on equality, promised Muslims the same opportunities as Hindus, Sikhs, Christians, Jains, Parsis, and Buddhists. But in practice, the distribution of opportunities depended on who was in power. Bigotry was a deep resource in the world's largest democracy, so political leaders built their careers by either patronizing religious minorities or marginalizing them. Since Hindu majoritarianism was in season, job applications from Muslim candidates were cheerfully tossed out.

Arif began to accept his fate at the truck business, shrinking in the presence of his short-tempered uncle, who refused to pay him a salary. "What for?" his uncle would bark, spit flying like shrapnel. "It's not enough that you eat like Tarzan?"

But as the Dosani family shop in the village tanked without capital to restock its inventory, and after his sister Farheen was pulled out of high school in preparation for marriage, Arif grew desperate. He cycled through a series of temp jobs—rolling cigarettes at a tobacco factory, selling mobile phone plans door-to-door, mopping floors and dusting cabinets at a pharmacy—but the work filled him with resentment. "I didn't come to Nagpur to work as a servant," Arif would tell Aunt Akida. "A job should have attitude."

One evening in the winter of 2014, smoking outside the corner hotel, Arif heard that the government, compelled by a bureaucratic obligation or a desire to correct its image, had introduced a minority youth employment scheme offering Muslim boys three thousand rupees ($50) to attend a training for police jobs.

◆┄┄┄◇┄┄┄➤

On his first day, Arif felt energized at the sight of the police training ground. It filled him with a maddening urge to consume the open field in big leaps, flying past boys who shuddered in the wind with their hollow ribs and matchstick legs. Suddenly he got the feeling that he was on the cusp of a fortuitous windfall.

A policeman's job, with its lifetime guaranteed salary insulated from the instability of economic downturns and changes in political regimes, was even better than a white-collar job, since the clout of government service would reverse the liability of his religious identity. Now *here* was a job with attitude.

But as soon as Arif's gaze turned toward a new batch of trainees, he felt himself shrink at the sight of beautiful young women training in the parade ground. Their tight braids swished above their small buttocks as they folded and unfolded their delicate bodies in and out of sun salutations, striking poses like erotic sculptures on the walls of ancient temples. Bhagyashri Ingle, a leonine beauty stretching her hips, scanned Arif from head to toe, her upper and lower halves churning at different speeds.

After the math lecture, Bhagyashri sashayed over to Arif's desk to ask how to calculate compound interest. She ignored his feeble mumbles, grabbed his phone, and added herself on Facebook. Even before he got home that evening, she had texted to ask if he would teach her math after class. At first, their private tutoring sessions took place in the lecture hall after it emptied out, but when murmurs began about a couple lingering behind to be alone together, they moved to a common friend's house.

A few days into their tutoring arrangement, Arif paid a roadside barber to give him the latest haircut—buzzed temples with a pelt of hair that swooshed upward—which he carefully sculpted while staring intently at his reflection in his bike's mirror. He shaved his stubble, showered himself in deodorant, and hung a pair of aviator sunglasses in the nook of a fresh shirt to complete a look that was, in his opinion, a statement of sophistication.

One afternoon, as Arif struggled to show Bhagyashri how to solve a profit-and-loss problem, she suddenly leaned forward and brushed his cheek. Later that night, after Arif had rubbed balm on his eyelids, then stuck his head in the air-conditioning vent of the next-door pharmacy to shock himself awake to study, Bhagyashri texted to ask if he had eaten dinner. From across the room, Aunt Akida shouted that she had never seen a boy smile so wide at a textbook.

However, a week later, when Arif asked Bhagyashri to be his girlfriend, she walked away without explanation. The realization that he had been revealing himself to a stranger jolted him awake from a deep slumber. Now it felt immature to ask for answers, especially since Bhagyashri acted like there had never been anything between them. *You can also be a flirter type*, he told himself. *What's stopping you?*

◆┈┈◇┈┈➤

One day, weeks later, Bhagyashri asked Arif to give her younger sister a lift. He took the opportunity to try out a new flirting routine. He slicked back his hair, dragged his motorbike to the gate, and throttled the engine. As they rode off, he shouted over the din of traffic, "I'm a simple guy from a village! I don't know how to talk to girls!" There was silence from the back seat. When Arif attempted a wheelie, the ritual of romantic subterfuge in small-town India, Monika Ingle, a young woman with the regal bearing of the Taj Mahal, sat tight like a precious touch-me-not.

The next time Bhagyashri brought her sister out to eat sweet roadside burgers known as *dabelis*, Monika's shrill voice flew out like a murder of crows. What was Arif staring at? Did he think he was the Bollywood hero Shah Rukh Khan? Had he smoked? Was he in the habit of trying his cheap tricks on every girl he saw? This woman, scolding him through a mouthful of *dabeli* he had paid for, was a firecracker. In the explosion of hysterical laughter, someone said that Arif and Monika would make a cute couple. Now Arif couldn't tear his eyes away from her. The way she tossed her hair and summoned mock horror for selfies sent electric currents through his body.

"This girl Monika has full-on attitude," Arif reported to his friend Akbar, who had also moved to Nagpur to work in a cigarette factory.

"Once you become a constable," Akbar said, "which girl in her right mind will say no to you?"

Arif couldn't put Monika out of his mind. He had seen beyond her beauty and into her shimmer-flecked eyes. There he had caught a deep sadness before she could hide it. Maybe she was in pain, or maybe she was stuck. Whatever it was, it made him certain she would be safe with no one other than him.

One afternoon, when Arif was driving past her library, he spotted Monika in tears. "Do you want to come with me?" he asked, skidding to a halt. She said no, she said yes, she said no again. Finally, she helped herself to the back seat, and he dropped her off at home without a word. Even as the city tore past them—a furious assault of cars, buses, crowds, cows—nothing existed except the woman on his motorbike.

"I don't know what made you cry, but I didn't like it," he texted her later.

"Take one advice from me: be with only one person till the end," she wrote back.

Arif really liked what she said. For a long time, he had harbored the suspicion that he was born to the wrong generation, especially when it came to matters of romantic attachment. The events with Bhagyashri had confirmed that women's hearts these days were cut too small and utilitarian to contain the extravagance of true love. Monika, with her lowered gaze and scolding, was different from the swarm of Bhagyashris.

With Monika, conversation came easy. It overflowed, spilling into hours, days, and weeks. Arif couldn't explain why he felt the

urge to delete her messages before class, except to avoid a need-
less interrogation from Bhagyashri. But when it became clear that
Monika was hiding their friendship from her sister too, they felt
like accomplices.

One monsoon evening, four months after they first met, Arif
drove Monika to the lakeside and pulled her close to ask her to be
his girlfriend.

"But you are Muslim." The words fell out of Monika's mouth
like loose change.

◄----◇----►

In 1940 Madhav Sadashiv Golwalkar, a zoology professor from a
village near Nagpur, took over the reins of the Rashtriya Swayamsevak Sangh, known simply as the Sangh, a Far Right quasi-militant
group devoted to the creation of a Hindu nation.

Hinduism is hard to distill into a binary, since, as a religious
practice, it is fluid, encompassing a bewildering plurality of gods,
castes, traditions, and philosophies. In Golwalkar's mind, it was
these inherent complexities and contradictions that made the Hindu
community vulnerable to centuries of foreign domination. Only a
Hindu society consolidated into a single force, he believed, could reverse India's decline from its glorious past.

Golwalkar, dour faced, with a chest-length beard and hard,
black eyes, found the model he was looking for in the Third Reich,
which was about to invade neighboring Poland, setting off the Second World War. "Germany has also shown how well-nigh impossible it is for races and cultures, having differences going to the root,
to be assimilated into one united whole," he wrote in his 1939 book

We or Our Nationhood Defined. "A good lesson for us in Hindusthan to learn and profit by."

In India, the races and cultures with differences going to the root were Hindus and Muslims, and therefore one definition of Hindu was "non-Muslim." As Golwalkar wrote in a later book, *Bunch of Thoughts* (1966), "whatever we believe in, the Muslim is wholly hostile to it. If we worship in the temple, he would desecrate it. If we carry on *bhajans* [devotional songs] and *rath yatras* [religious processions], that would irritate him. If we worship the cow, he would like to eat it. If we glorify the woman as a symbol of sacred motherhood, he would like to molest her." The Hindutva ideology, a hypermasculine form of Hindu nationalism propagated by the Sangh, required Muslims to accept a Hindu cultural identity and remain subordinate to a Hindu nation.

When Golwalkar took charge of the Sangh in 1940, the call for independence from British rule, led by Mohandas Karamchand Gandhi, was sweeping the country. Gandhi began his morning lectures quoting Hindu scriptures from the Bhagavad Gita, alongside passages from the Bible and the Quran, and talked about a new nation where every religion would enjoy equal respect. The Sangh's leadership, irked by Gandhi for "giving no thought to protecting Hindu culture and Hindu dharma," opted out of the national movement, insisting that Hindu society was under siege, not from British occupation but from India's own Muslims and Christians.

By the time the leader of the political group All India Muslim League, Mohammed Ali Jinnah, had popularized the demand for a separate Muslim homeland called Pakistan, Golwalkar had expanded his mission of building a Hindu nation in India beyond the borders of Nagpur, creating a network of allied organizations under the umbrella of the Sangh Parivar, a family of Hindu nationalists. With the Sangh's patronage, millions of men in khaki shorts and white shirts received paramilitary training to prepare for a revival of Hindu glory.

In 1947 a British lawyer named Cyril Radcliffe arrived in colonial India with the task of drawing a border across the Punjab and Bengal Provinces to divide the subcontinent into Muslim-majority Pakistan and Hindu-majority India. With Britain in tatters after World War II, Radcliffe had just five weeks to complete the job of decolonization while nursing a bout of dysentery. It was also his first time setting foot in India.

After the new borders were announced, roughly fourteen million people suddenly found themselves on the wrong side, setting off cyclones of communal violence that killed one million and uprooted twelve million others. Radcliffe burned his papers, rejected his fee, and sailed back to Britain. The Radcliffe Line, as the border between two enemy states came to be known, turned into a heaving wound of hostility between Hindus and Muslims.

A month later, in September 1947, Gandhi confronted Golwalkar about the Sangh's role in inciting communal violence. He argued that independent India was a secular democracy that belonged equally to Hindus and Muslims. Even as Golwalkar assured Gandhi that the Sangh was a peaceful organization and did not stand for the killing of Muslims, Gandhi remained unconvinced.

"I have heard it said that the Sangh is at the root of all this mischief," Gandhi said in a speech in November. "Hinduism cannot be saved by orgies of murder." On the evening of January 30, 1948,

Nathuram Godse, a former cadre of the Sangh, walked into a prayer meeting and pumped three bullets point-blank into Gandhi's chest.

A decade later, in another part of western India, an eight-year-old boy named Narendra Modi, who sold tea at the Vadnagar railway station, attended his first lecture at the Sangh's local office. He took a vow of celibacy to dedicate his life to the organization, rising through its ranks—first as junior cadet, then as regional organizer, and eventually as a prime ministerial candidate of the Bharatiya Janata Party, the political wing of the Sangh acquiesced to its Hindutva ideology.

◆━━◇━━◆

In present-day Nagpur, Golwalkar's ghost presided over every messy intricacy of daily life. When Arif passed through Reshimbagh, the thriving Hindu neighborhood where Monika grew up, his body stiffened with fear that someone would grab his collar and begin thrashing him. It was here, where housewives in puff-sleeved nighties haggled cheerfully at vegetable carts, that a Hindu-Muslim riot ignited by a Sangh procession had reaped its first harvest of lives a half century earlier. Since then, the same violence had visited again and again. It was there, three lanes over from Monika's house, that Golwalkar's last rites were performed, in 1973. In that sprawling compound, an annual summer camp continued to prepare thousands for a Hindu reawakening. The Sangh's cadres stomped like soldiers, arranged in neat columns and trailing a marching band, like a state cavalcade. Nagpur's map was blotches of saffron and green, with the city organized into Hindu and Muslim pockets; into Reshimbaghs of Monikas and Hasanbaghs of Arifs.

That evening, when Monika offered Arif his Muslim identity
as an explanation for her rejection, the happy kingdom of delusions
he had built for himself shattered like a dropped mirror. "History
is witness that Hindus and Muslims cannot be together," Arif told
his old friend Khaled on the phone. "If we are snakes, they are
mongooses."

Two weeks later, when Arif's worldly pragmatism had dissolved into
the despair of one-sided love, Monika accepted a platonic invitation
to go see the Hindi movie *Hamari Adhuri Kahani* (in English, *Our
Incomplete Story*). The actor Emraan Hashmi appeared on-screen,
accusing the woman he pursued of secretly loving him back, as Arif
searched Monika's face in the darkness of the matinee show. "You
love me, but you won't say it," Hashmi's character said, and Arif
cleared his throat to emphasize that this was a movie about their
own lives. "You want to fall into my embrace, you want to stay in my
heart, but you won't allow it," the actor went on. That's when Arif
saw Monika clench a smile.

When they walked out from the movie theater into the sun blast
of the street, the tense silence between them sounded like two held
breaths. The movie's ending was tragic, with both Hashmi and his
love interest dead, confirming the suspicion that two forbidden lovers could find eternal bliss only in death.

"Look, I am in this field for a long time," Arif said, referring
to the field of romantic pursuit. He opened the conversation asking her to date him in the same way he began requests for pocket
money, passing marks in school, a cigarette, or a transfer of mobile

talk time. "Please, *yaar*. I'll treat you like a queen," he said, his face crumpled like a discarded love letter. "Only one chance. Don't I deserve that much?"

"Okay," he heard her say before she disappeared into Reshimbagh.

Chapter 4

Right Wrong, Wrong Right

T o Monika Ingle's surprise, Mohammad Arif Dosani fit nicely into her life, with only minor alterations to her daily rituals. Before leaving for college, for instance, she tossed a scarf into her purse to cover her face in case their romantic bike rides took them through crowded junctions in a city where everyone knew everyone. On Mondays, Wednesdays, and Fridays, after helping the neighbor's children with their homework, she lingered outside for an extra minute so Arif could feast his eyes from the tea shop across the street. At night, she borrowed her father's phone to download the lyrics of movie songs and ended up locking herself in the bathroom to scroll through the hundreds of private messages he left her on Facebook.

Once Arif had filled the vacancy of a boyfriend in Monika's life, checking off the main requirements of being hot and cool, she didn't give her choice much thought. Sometimes, watching movies about the enormity of love, her life felt like a hollow shell without him. After seeing *Hamari Adhuri Kahani*, for instance, she noticed his light-brown eyes for the first time. After another movie date, to see the historical drama *Bajirao Mastani*, she appreciated how defined his shoulders were.

But most of the time, she existed in a suspended state of guilt or innocence, discovering slowly how poorly suited she was to conducting a secret love affair. Up until now, Monika had thrilled in small and reasonable acts of freedom, such as leaving home in a tunic then changing into a sleeveless top in the college bathroom, or splurging her Diwali and Rakhi savings on ice cream. But this business of making a boyfriend vanish under a cloak of deceit was too burdensome. Apart from the demanding logistics of inventing excuses and alibis, it made her sad that the lies that left her mouth so freely were gradually moving her away from her mother, father, sister, and brother. Her only confidant now was a stranger named Mohammad Arif Dosani.

Whenever Monika found herself in one of these contemplative moods, she suddenly concluded that the whole thing with Arif was moving too fast. Especially when he spoke with finality, saying, for example, that she was the future wife for whom he was struggling to become a policeman. His jokes would annoy her, his loud chewing would disgust her, his grubby fingernails would irk her, and she would call off the relationship. Arif would wait for a day to pass, for her mood to settle, and she would allow him once again to persuade her to give it another try.

A few months into their relationship, one summer evening in 2015, after a marathon viewing of *Emotional Atyachar*, a hidden-camera reality TV show about cheating partners, Monika acquired a heightened sense of awareness. Arif appeared to be perfectly content with their bare-minimum romantic arrangement, as agreeable to holding her hand in the park as he was to swallowing the indignity of her whimsical silences. This made her suspicious, since the show had alerted her to a full catalogue of crimes committed by boyfriends who appeared to be too accommodating.

A few nights later, Monika found the evidence she was looking for when her sister Bhagyashri's laughter dribbled into their room. "Arif . . ." Her sister said the name with a vulgar familiarity that tore into Monika's skin like a hastily fastened zipper. Bhagyashri told Monika she had taken Arif's aunt Akida to the eye doctor for her cataract treatment and spent the rest of the afternoon soaking in sweet stories about Arif's childhood. As she watched her sister fall into bed, giggling at the chubby baby Arif was, Monika's heart thumped wildly with panic.

A suspicion had fluttered into Monika's mind weeks earlier, when she noticed Bhagyashri's face burn when friends teased her and Arif together. Later, Monika heard her sister praise Arif's dedication to his police career and noticed how serious she had become about her own training. Bhagyashri suddenly began praying to a Sufi saint whose shrine Arif visited. Now, a full picture began to form in Monika's mind: Bhagyashri harbored feelings for Arif.

The next day, one afternoon in July 2015, Monika asked Arif to meet her at a restaurant so that they could break up, and she could advise him to date her sister instead. Before their meeting, she dangled a razor blade over her wrist, in a half-hearted display of despair appropriate for a woman who was giving up her boyfriend for the sake of her sister. Then she put away the blade carefully. This was also a tranquil forsaking because she could no longer bear the burden of skulking and hiding.

"Do you think you're some goddess of sacrifice?" Arif looked at her in disbelief. "You're the goddess, and I'm the sacrificial lamb?"

"Bhaga and you are perfect for each other," Monika said. "You two can be happy together." She waited for the tears to come, but her eyes were still dry.

"Is this a joke?" Arif asked. "What will I do in a love triangle with Bhaga and her boyfriends?"

"She likes you."

"I like *you*."

"But she likes you."

"But I like you!"

Monika caught Arif's tear-glistened cheeks in the neon glow of the restaurant's fish tank. This was not the first time Arif had told her he liked her, but it was the first time his words meant something to her. For the entirety of her young life, Monika had allowed her sister's desires to take precedence over her own. If Monika received an envelope stuffed with cash on her birthday, she expected Bhagyashri to be standing behind her, palm out. If Bhagyashri fancied a dress that belonged to Monika, she was capable of tearing it to shreds.

Everyone said that Bhagyashri had inherited the big personality of their father, Shridhar Ingle, a man who had grown a small empire of double cotton mattresses. They also said that Monika had inherited their mother's silence; Ranjana was a homemaker who put her family's needs before her own. Monika had tethered her personality to this truth as she grew up in the shadow of her sister, floating through life, never willing things to happen, only accepting them as part of her karma, until she had lost the habit of thinking of herself at all. For the first time in an eternity, Monika let it sink in that someone was choosing her over Bhagyashri.

⟵----◇----⟶

In July 2016, more than a year into their relationship, on Bakri Eid, the holiest day in the Islamic calendar, Arif turned up at police training in a new white shirt with gray polka dots. "Look at a lion's face," he said as he strode into class, popping his collar and rolling up his sleeves. "Not his new shirt, *chaka-chak*," sparkling clean. Arif was in top form, hilarious and unstoppable, but something about the shirt bothered Bhagyashri. The hunch that she had seen it before followed her all day, until she returned home and saw a crumpled shopping bag in Monika's cupboard.

A few days later, when Monika was rushing out for college, Bhagyashri noticed that a pen had leaked inside her bag and stained the front flap. That afternoon, at training, Bhagyashri saw a similar ink stain on Arif's clothes.

Later that evening, Bhagyashri grabbed her sister by the elbow, dragged her to the terrace, and began slapping her. A religious procession was surging through the street below, with prancing men trailing an enormous idol of the elephant-headed Lord Ganesh, studded with gemstones, dusted in gold, laden with necklaces, traveling through Reshimbagh on a pickup truck fitted with strobe lights.

"Arif and you!" Bhagyashri screamed as if she were the one being physically assaulted. The commotion of the procession drowned out her voice, and her mother, oblivious, continued preparing dinner downstairs. "You two! There is something between you two!" Bhagyashri moaned. Her eyes looked like they would crack open with rage, her words started to garble into grunts, and when she heard Monika say again and again there was nothing between them, she suddenly turned to the wall and started punching it. Monika froze, watching her sister unravel in the theatrics of her own making, waiting for the performance to reach its denouement.

"If there is something between Arif and you, you will tell me?" Bhagyashri asked as she took Monika's face in her hands.

"Promise," Monika sobbed, but neither she nor her sister believed her lie.

After that night, everything changed. The happy home of Monika's childhood began closing in on her like a cage. It started with Monika suspecting that Bhagyashri followed her to college to catch her red-handed with Arif. Slowly, she came to realize that her sister had a rotating cast of friends to keep an eye on her. Their mother suddenly insisted on knowing who Monika was chatting with on the phone and followed her out to see if she was really going to the neighbor's house to help with their children's homework. But what really hurt, and what Monika detested Bhagyashri for, was the punishing silence that draped itself over every inch of the house.

One afternoon in April 2017, Monika left home for college and went to meet Arif. As she climbed the stairs to the empty flat Arif had borrowed from a friend for the date, she focused her attention on keeping her face still as he loomed into view. Arif stood in the doorway in an undershirt and pajamas, the way he usually was at home, winking at her from across the hall.

The last time they had met in this flat, they had spent the afternoon sitting awkwardly on opposite ends of the bed in a delicate silence that stretched too long. Luckily, a little girl from the neighboring flat had accidentally run inside and broken the spell. Monika had scooped up the girl, plonked her in her lap, and fed her a packet of biscuits.

Today's silence was charged with a wounded affection. Suddenly everything except Arif blurred and faded like a movie scene. When he bolted the door shut, one half of her felt terrified by what she had set in motion even as the other half expected a romantic song to begin playing.

◆┄┄◇┄┄▶

The day the monsoon season broke above Nagpur, Monika woke up covered in sweat. Her chest felt tight, her head spun, her legs cramped, and a sour stink rose from her body. The first thought that entered her mind left her numb with fear, so she called Arif to confirm that she had not dreamed up taking an emergency contraceptive on the way home from his friend's flat. Finally, satisfied with his corroboration, she swallowed the fear with a painkiller.

Weeks went by, and now when the fear rose in her throat, she pushed it down with bowlfuls of papaya, coffee, and raw eggs produced by a sacred breed of black-feathered chicken—mends to induce menstrual bleeding, which she learned from soap operas. Another fortnight passed, with the new diet producing nothing except two new wretched pimples, and Monika told Arif to get abortion pills.

One morning in July 2017, when her father studied the electricity bill with the same suspicion that he viewed it with every month, she offered to accompany him to the power distribution office. Since Monika had twice succeeded in getting the bill halved by giving a clerk the full benefit of her smile, her father nodded at her suggestion and took a last gulp of tea. Before leaving home, she texted Arif to bring the pills.

When Shridhar was pulled into a negotiation at the power company, Monika wandered outside, pretending to go looking for a missing earring, but her father's gaze followed her through the glass door of the office, losing her in the blur of the street and then finding her again, talking to a strange man. When they got home, Shridhar broke into a rage, faulting his wife for her loose grip on the girls. Ranjana decided that Monika would no longer leave the house alone.

While her parents argued, Monika swallowed the abortion pills in the bathroom, searching her amused face in the mirror, relishing the idea that the recent turn of events would have been explosive in a daily soap. She sat down on the floor and texted Arif a line of dialogue from a Hindi movie: "Okay, so who are you of mine?"

"I'm scared about what you will say . . ." he wrote back.

"Hmm, then listen," she wrote. "Arif is my life . . . something which I can't express in words."

"Wow, me shock and you totally rock," he replied.

That night, they stayed up until dawn, making plans and imagining their future together. After three or four years, once Bhagyashri was married and Arif was settled in his police job, they would ask their parents for permission to marry.

"When will Bhaga get married, *yaar*?" Arif asked longingly.

Two weeks later, in August, Monika called Arif to instruct him to make a doctor's appointment because there was still no sign of her period. The clinic was a small room with yellow walls, a swing door, a washbasin the color of a decaying tooth, a shelf stacked full of tubes and bottles, a trolley with a knot of wires, and an examination table smeared with hair oil.

The doctor, a woman with sharp eyes set inside rimless spectacles, refused to move a facial muscle for the eternity Arif took to explain their situation. "No marriage?" she asked. "How can you people be so stupid?"

From the moment Monika's ultrasound exam began, the minutes moved so slowly that it felt as if time had lost its purpose—and when the diagnosis came, it somehow froze. Monika was sixteen weeks and five days pregnant. Even though Indian law permitted abortions, social stigma made doctors reluctant to perform the surgery, especially for unmarried couples. Monika lifted her head, surveyed Arif's blank face, the shabby clinic, the humiliating interrogation. This was the deplorable world her recklessness had pushed her into.

"I know a clinic that will do our work," Arif said after they stepped out of the doctor's office. "My friend also had the same problem, and it went away."

"What will I do now?" Monika said, not listening. "I will have to die."

"It's a very simple operation," Arif went on. "No one will even come to know."

◆━━━◆━━━▶

On a Sunday afternoon, Monika stayed in bed, overhearing snatches of a show from the living room. In today's episode of *Aap Ki Adalat* (*The People's Court*), a new chief minister named Yogi Adityanath was in the television courtroom's witness box. Adityanath, the head priest of a Hindu temple in northern India who began his political career as a Sangh activist, had recently emerged from obscurity as Prime Minister Narendra Modi's pick to lead India's largest state, Uttar Pradesh, a post seen as a launching pad for the country's highest office.

In this rerun of an old interview, recorded three years before he was named chief minister and became careful to avoid controversial statements, Adityanath lamented an existential crisis threatening the fabric of Hindu society. He described the inner workings of an evil design known as "love jihad," in which Muslim men seduced Hindu women with the single aim of getting them pregnant in order to water down the country's Hindu majority. Adityanath, who had devoted a third of his life to investigating love jihad, believed an anonymous syndicate of international terror groups incentivized Muslim men to brainwash Hindu women with false promises of love, to establish an Islamic caliphate in the subcontinent.

"Love jihad is an international conspiracy against our country and our country's culture," he declared. "I'm not the only one saying this . . . Uttar Pradesh High Court in 2006 instructed the state to investigate why so many Hindu girls were being kidnapped . . . in 2009 Kerala High Court asked why more than five thousands Hindu girls were abducted in less than four years . . . Karnataka High Court issued a similar order asking why this matter is not being investigated by the Criminal Investigation Department. Where are these Hindu girls disappearing suddenly? We will not allow this evil in the name of jihad to take root in India."

Every Valentine's Day, a procession of sword-wielding street fighters of the Bajrang Dal, a youth affiliate of the Sangh, passed through Reshimbagh, alerting Hindu families to the danger of Muslim boys lurking outside colleges to seduce Hindu girls. The processions were always a festive display of creativity: one year, demonstrators set fire to heart-shaped pillows and teddy bears; another year, they paraded donkeys wearing wedding garlands.

Back on the TV in the other room, the interviewer interrupted the chief minister to ask a question. "Yogi-ji, have you ever been in love?"

"I am an ascetic," he replied with a smile. "I only love Mother India."

"If you have never been in love, how would you know that when you exchange hearts, you cannot ask for a curriculum vitae?"

"Marriage is the foundation stone on which our nation is built," he maintained. "If the foundation is wrong, the nation will come tumbling." As Monika's living room echoed with applause, a knot formed in her stomach as she reminded herself that Arif was a Muslim man, and she was a Hindu woman. *What was the future for such a match?*

◆┄┄◇┄┄▶

In the weeks after Monika's ultrasound, Arif identified clinics across the region that could be persuaded to perform abortions. But the end to all his worries lay beyond one final obstacle: How would his girlfriend make her way to the facility and spend the night there without her family's knowledge?

"What will I tell my family?" she asked. "There is no way I can stay overnight at the hospital."

"I've been running all over the province begging doctors to perform the surgery to get us out of this problem," Arif said. "And you are worried about what you will say at home?"

"There must be some way the operation can happen without staying overnight," Monika sobbed. "What will I tell my mother?"

On one hand, Monika kept saying she would die if the pregnancy was not terminated, and on the other hand, now that Arif had arranged everything, she suddenly backed out. For a moment, Arif wondered if it was possible that she wanted to carry the baby to term, but he told himself that she was too scared to think clearly.

In the past days, Arif had himself struggled to understand his own ideas of right and wrong. *Would it be right to kill a baby in the womb? Would it be wrong to let the baby live and destroy so many lives? Would it be wrong to run away and let Monika face the consequences if that meant saving his dreams? Would it be right to marry her even if he was not ready?*

"What should I do?" Arif asked Khaled.

"Look out for yourself," his friend advised "Her family is there to look after her."

Arif tried to see the pragmatism in the advice, but it made him sick to his stomach. "For the first time in my life, the antenna of my brain and my heart are both out of coverage area," he said. "What is right? What is wrong?"

As days passed, Monika feared she would lose her mind from worrying. When tunics that once hung loose on her frame started getting snug, she became wild with panic, trying so hard to squeeze into them that she ended up in hysterical tears, panting and sweating. When her feet broke into pregnancy rashes, she scratched them until they bled. Once, when Bhagyashri casually asked if she was unwell, Monika could not sleep for days, dreaming up apocalyptic scenarios of her sister dragging her to the doctor and ordering a sonogram. Suddenly Monika would feel so restless that her legs would begin twitching. She would start shaking them violently to make the twitching stop and end up in another fit of uncontrollable tears.

The longer she stayed at home, she knew, the harder it would get to keep her pregnancy a secret. Her family would decide to pay their way through an abortion, but they were sure to keep her shame burning with their silence. Their silence would ask the same questions again and again until she would surely go mad: Why did she do this? Where did they go wrong? What did they do to deserve it? Wasn't she their good daughter?

"Don't do something stupid with yourself," Arif texted Monika when he started to worry that she was experiencing suicidal thoughts.

"I have two options," Monika wrote back. "Either I commit suicide, or I go away with you.

"Can you arrange everything? Can we get married tomorrow?" she added a moment later.

"Send me your documents," he wrote back. "I'll find a marriage lawyer."

◆┈┈◇┈┈▶

A few days later, Arif arrived at the civil court to meet an attorney whose phone number popped up on Google. Before the appointment, he had researched an interfaith marriage law called the Special Marriage Act of 1954, which the great founders of India had snuck into the legal framework of a country governed by separate marriage laws based on religious scriptures and beliefs. The Hindu Marriage Act, enacted the following year, for Hindus, was based on their beliefs, while the 1937 Muslim Personal Law, or Shariat, grounded in Islamic beliefs, was for Muslims.

The Special Marriage Act stood as the only legal way for a Hindu to marry a Muslim without converting. When Arif brought this up with his lawyer, Vilas Dongre twisted his face as if he had swallowed a tamarind popsicle. "Let me ask you a simple question: Do you want to get screwed?" he asked with genuine curiosity. Marriage officers were required to give the public a month to file objections before an interfaith marriage could be solemnized, he explained.

This was often more than enough time for disapproving families to coerce the bride and groom out of their decision.

Dongre's legal counsel, at the cost of eight thousand rupees ($110), was to convert Monika to Islam and marry in a mosque. After the religious ceremony known as a *nikah*, the lawyer would send copies of their marriage certificate to the local police station. That way, even if their parents objected to the marriage, they would not be able to force them to separate.

"Go away for a few hours after they get to know about your wedding," Dongre advised. In a majority of the cases, he said, families grew tired of fighting once a marriage was legally solemnized. "By the evening, her parents will be feeding you sweets."

One afternoon in August, when no one was home except Monika and her mother, a college classmate arrived with a stack of books to help Monika catch up on missed lectures. As Ranjana bustled around in the kitchen, the classmate—who was really a friend of Arif's—spread out a sheaf of papers on the counter and noted that it would be easier to photocopy the coursework at a corner shop. Between her onions turning black and the dripping dish sponge in her hand, Ranjana nodded them off.

That afternoon, Monika and Arif signed their marriage papers in the living room of a Muslim cleric as his wife cooked lunch inside. Monika converted to Islam, and they married. When they left the cleric's house, Monika Ingle had become Ayat Mohammad Arif Dosani. Ayat, an Arabic name picked out by Arif, referred to the holy verses of the Quran. He was twenty-five, and she, twenty.

Days before Monika and Arif were to leave home, a bride-viewing party for Bhagyashri settled into her family's living room. Ranjana skittered around the kitchen, sari hitched up to her ankles, hastily sliding vegetable-filled pastries called samosas into a pan of whistling oil as Shridhar gently scolded the guests to fill up their plates. Bhagyashri sat in a plastic chair, face caked with makeup, paddling her feet under a chiffon sari. The prospective groom, a railway clerk from the same caste, asked the young woman her hobbies, and she answered coyly that she liked to watch movies, as the elders nodded good-naturedly. Monika caught herself wishing, as if by habit, that it was she and not Bhagyashri who had been lucky enough to find a husband loved by her parents.

The night before she was to leave, Monika followed her parents to their room to tell her mother she was craving *idlis*, the steamed rice cakes her mother made on special occasions. She flopped into bed between her parents, laying her head in her father's lap, and watched her mother coil her long hair into a thick bun. When she wished them good night, she hugged them tight, as if she were imprinting herself onto them.

At dawn on August 29, 2017, as the sky turned from pitch black to deep purple, Monika unlatched the main door of her house and threw a suitcase over the ledge. Four hours later, she stepped into her slippers and walked out, as the idlis whistled in a steamer.

Chapter 5

I Am Reshma

The day after her grandmother died suddenly on a hot summer day in 2017, Reshma Mokenwar stretched out in front of
the family television. She was a twenty-eight-year-old sales assistant from Mumbai with a heart-shaped face stained yellow from
a lifetime of turmeric fairness treatments and a tongue sharpened
through the knife grinder of a bad marriage.

Secretly, Reshma was thrilled that her grandmother was finally
burning in a hell that, for once, was not of her own making. But the
old woman's crumbling home in Chikhali, a godforsaken village on
the border of the states of Telangana and Maharashtra, filled her
with gloom even on good days like these.

As her mother, sisters, and aunts covered their heads with the
folds of their white saris and squatted by the door to receive condo-
lences, Reshma drifted in and out of sleep under the spell of television home shopping commercials.

She closed her eyes, pictured a door, and waited for it to open. After a while, when no one materialized, she grunted and turned over to reboot the dream. This time she saw eyes that burned with the luminosity of a thousand suns and tasted a scent that was the earth after it had rained. Preethi Sarikela, an eighteen-year-old daughter of her father's cousin sister from the village who was stretched out on the bed beside her, shifted a lock of hair from her face and smiled. Even though Reshma had never met this girl before, it was Preethi who felt like her own in a room full of familiar faces.

"You girls have any shame?" An uncle's voice boomed from outside the dreamy fog. "Want me to beat it into you?" Preethi's eyes clouded with embarrassment, and she untangled herself from Reshma to make tea for a new flock of relatives at the door.

Years earlier, when Reshma found herself alone on the ground of a cotton field contemplating suicide, she had asked herself how much of her was alive and received no reply. Days later, when she woke up on a hospital bed, she vowed to never give up another opportunity to live. Now she followed Preethi to the kitchen and tapped her shoulder. "I am Reshma," she said. "Did you feel a fire between us?"

◆━━◇━━◆

Twenty-eight years earlier, in 1989, when Reshma was born in a filthy public hospital in the Mumbai suburb of Mulund, her mother, Rekha, sat up in a tattered nightgown and a halo of frizz to grieve the birth of a third daughter instead of a prized first son. She beat her chest, tore her hair, and howled until she passed out.

When her eyes opened in the darkness before dawn, an angelic nurse appeared with a pocket-sized photograph of Lord Ganesh, the elephant-headed destroyer of obstacles, and instructed her to tuck it under her pillow. Miraculously, two years later, Reshma's mother gave birth to a son she and her husband would name Ganesh.

The next year, Rekha focused her thoughts on Lord Krishna, an incarnation of the protector of the universe, and, once again, her prayers were answered with a son named Kishen. There were enough Hindu gods, approximately thirty-three million, to keep praying to for male children until she had finally won over the affection of her mother-in-law, but after her middle daughter, Kanchan, suddenly stopped breathing, it became necessary to think about keeping the rest of her four hungry children alive.

Half her husband's salary from his driving job went straight to his mother in Chikhali and the other half went down the drain with his drunken vomit. One night, when Reshma's father, Babu Mokenwar, came home to Friends Colony, a hive of identical rooms in the ruins of Bhandup village, swaying like a treetop in the Mumbai monsoon, Rekha told him she had picked up a job cleaning dirty dishes in a nearby apartment high-rise. He nodded, still splayed belly down, caught up in a weak-lunged debate with his own ghosts. Day after day, Reshma's mother fed her children leftovers she collected in ratty plastic bags, but the sounds of their rumbling bellies kept growing louder and louder.

One afternoon, Rekha stuffed a schoolbag with frocks and sent her eldest daughter, Pinki, to live in Chikhali. Under her grandmother's supervision, Pinki blossomed into a model of unquestioning obedience, a beautiful young woman capable of cultivating cotton and rice in a barren desert and changing the destiny of any kitchen she made her own. When it was time to start looking for matches in the extended family, suitors poured in from both the matrilineal and patrilineal lines. In the part of Telangana the Mokenwars belonged to, marriage between parallel cousins, or children of two cousins of the same sex, is considered incest, but marriage between cross-cousins, or children of two cousins of the opposite sex, is a cherished observance. Before Reshma's mother had a chance to worry, Pinki was happily married and settled in the farming village of Pochera, five hundred miles from Mumbai.

It was her younger daughter she lost sleep over. Not only was Reshma heavy and dark skinned, but she was also hotheaded and stubborn. At thirteen and in fifth grade, when Reshma's breasts began to grow, her father noticed that she walked with her chest thrown out in a group full of girls with stooped shoulders. "You are a girl!" he barked and slapped her shoulders to make her hunch. "So learn to act like a girl."

One monsoon evening in 2002, during her favorite time of the year, Reshma saw her mother stuffing a schoolbag with her frocks. The neighborhood's winding bylanes were strung up with color-changing fairy lights, and the whole neighborhood thundered with music for the Hindu festival of Navratri. She threw herself at her mother and protested, "I want to study. I don't want to go to the village."

As villages and towns flew past her train window on the overnight journey to her grandmother's house in Chikhali, she stared silently into the darkness, hot tears stinging her eyes, thinking about how her sister Pinki left and never returned.

Despite regular beatings from her grandmother, Reshma never grew tired of provoking her. When the old woman stood hunched over the vendors' scales and weights, drooling from the corners of her mouth, muttering her usual laments about how her old bones still toiled in scorching fields to support her son's family, Reshma dropped a heavy bale of cotton on her foot to teach her a lesson. When the woman sent her out to buy small bottles of cloudy country liquor, Reshma gleefully made it trickle down the dirt road crowded with herds of scavenging donkeys. By the end of the first year, Reshma had mastered a wicked imitation of her grandmother hobbling through the fields, head bobbing, arms windmilling, but there was no one except two even-tempered bulls to vouch for its accuracy.

"You never tell the old witch to behave herself," Reshma complained to her mother from the coin-box phone on the street corner. "Do you even know the kind of dirty swear words that come out of her mouth?"

In a small corner of Reshma's heart was the hope that her grandmother would eventually tire of her and send her back home to Bhandup, and everything would be restored to its proper place. Years passed, Navratris came and went, her brothers went from middle school to high school, the Friends Colony house got a new lick of bright yellow paint, and Reshma felt foolish still dreaming about the day she would leave her grandmother's village.

On Reshma's seventeenth birthday, when Pinki brought her a marriage proposal, the family leapt at the opportunity, fearing there would not be another. A farmhand who lived two doors from Pinki's home in Pochera was willing to marry Reshma in exchange for the reasonable dowry of ten thousand rupees ($150). Reshma, tempted by the prospect of leaving her grandmother, allowed the arrangements to proceed.

◆┄┄◇┄┄◆

On the night of their wedding, Reshma didn't want her husband to touch her. When he slipped his hand inside her blouse, she threatened to break his arm and throw it to a pack of dogs. He slapped her, told her to lay down as instructed, and climbed on top of her. When he grew tired of her protests, he buried his head in her chest and kept moving. The next morning, Reshma went to work in her husband's place in the cotton fields while he blew his dowry money in jugs at the corner liquor shop.

"Don't think too much," Reshma's mother told her on the phone when she sensed her disquietude. "It's a bad habit."

Night after night, Reshma lay in the stench of her husband and tried to make sense of the anger, shame, disgust, and betrayal that consumed her when his ragged nails tore into her skin like a rusted farm sickle. She reminded herself of her mother and clenched her eyes shut to quit the bad habit of thinking too much. She saw the low-ceilinged home of her childhood in Friends Colony. A termite-proof shrine of Lord Ganesh and Lord Krishna fitted with a disco ball and an electric candle. The pink-and-yellow peplum frock of her school days. Her mother's small hands. An overturned dinner plate. A dangling water pipe. Suddenly the silent images came alive, and she started to shake with anger. She saw herself as a child, crashing into her father, kicking him, biting him, punching him, and shouting at him to leave her mother alone. She saw him dashing around madly, flogging Rekha with a rubber hose, and her eyes filled with tears.

When Reshma looked into the mirror, she saw glimpses of her mother, and a familiar wave of confused anger broke inside her. *Why did her mother bring her father a cup of tea for his headache after he had brutally beaten her the night before? And why did she bring her husband a cup of tea the morning after she felt that he had forced himself on her?*

Those days, whenever Reshma talked to her mother, she could tell that whatever Rekha said to her was an echo of something her brothers and father wanted her to know:

"Your father is working overtime at the driving job to repay the loan he took for your dowry."

"Your brother Ganesh has rented out his two taxis because he is still burdened with bills from your wedding."

"Your brother Kishen has crushed his political ambitions and become a bank clerk to help out with household expenses."

One day Reshma finally snapped. "A woman should leave her parents' house in a palanquin and return only in a bier," she said sharply. "That is what you want to tell me?"

One night in 2013, days after their sixth wedding anniversary, Reshma's husband dragged her to a shack in the landlord's cotton field in a fit of drunken rage. Why did she not want him to touch her? Was she sleeping with her brother-in-law? Did he satisfy her after he satisfied her sister? Reshma looked up at the sky, saw the skeletons of cotton stalks swaying in a pale moonlight, and it occurred to her that she wanted to be free. She emptied a bottle of pesticide into her mouth, stared back into her husband's bloodshot eyes, and wiped her lips.

<hr />

"I am Reshma," she said to Preethi in her grandmother's kitchen four years after she climbed out of a hospital bed and walked out on her husband for good. "Do you also feel there is a fire between us?"

The clatter of teacups in Preethi's hands stopped.

"Yes," came a bell-clear reply.

For the next thirteen days, during the time it was said to take for her grandmother's soul to break free from her mortal remains and transcend into the universe, according to Hindu funeral customs, Reshma and Preethi became fused into each other.

They wandered off on long walks together, fell into stacks of hay, sang songs, and felt the sun on their faces. Reshma braided Preethi's hair. Preethi shaped Reshma's eyebrows. When they made love, they let their bodies come alive.

So far, Reshma had floated through life, never willing the direction she was going in. Now, in Preethi's company, she was starting to feel her heels finally digging into the earth. In their short time together, Reshma came to know a happiness that permeated her deepest memories and allowed her to finally grieve them.

One afternoon, resting her head in Preethi's lap, Reshma narrated a sequence of dialogues she had recently memorized from a TV show called *The 'Other' Love Story*. "This world, these rules, the unseen society, binding love, incomprehensible relationships, must-do obligations, the order, the rights and the wrongs of the conditioned mind. All this on one side," Reshma told Preethi. "The look in your eyes when you look at me, that touch in your hand when you hold me, that word on the tip of your tongue which stays unsaid, and that sigh which gets heavy when we move closer." Preethi paused to listen carefully, and Reshma continued: "That magnetic energy that gets created when we share the same space. And that tremble which gets etched on our beings when we move away. All this on the other side."

◆┄┄◇┄┄➤

On the thirteenth day of Reshma's grandmother's wake, when the extended family prepared to disperse back to their towns and villages across Maharashtra and Telangana, Preethi's eyes swept across the room and rested on Reshma in a silent accusation. Was she just going to watch and allow them to go their separate ways?

Reshma ran up to Preethi's mother and took the bags from her hand. "Let me carry those for you," she said. "Your knees must be hurting." Narsa, a scrawny woman hunched from a lifetime of picking cotton, doddered behind, listening eagerly as Reshma exaggerated her experience as a sales assistant at Patanjali Ayurved, a chain of shops selling Ayurvedic medicines invented by a famous yoga guru, Baba Ramdev.

"Ginger and root pepper are good for joint pain," Reshma said to Narsa as she helped her climb into the minibus headed for their village. "If you have any pain, call me, and I'll make it all vanish." As the bus turned, Reshma ran up to Preethi's window and winked, hinting that she had figured out a plan for them to see each other again.

Days later, Reshma appeared at Preethi's doorstep in Bazarhathnoor, a farming village five hundred miles from Mumbai, carrying a bag stuffed with the Patanjali Ayurvedic medicines she had recommended to Narsa. As Reshma pulled out fairness creams, oils, face packs, shampoos, and conditioners, Preethi, bubbling with laughter, stood in the corridor and watched her mother's face light up.

"Have you met Baba Ramdev?" Narsa wanted to know. The influential guru, who appeared in a saffron loincloth on television screens across the countryside, claimed to harness ancient Indian wisdom into affordable cures for diabetes, hypertension, baldness, heart problems, impotence, cancer, and homosexuality.

◆━━◇━━◆

From the moment Reshma stepped into Preethi's house, she made herself at home, a useful strategy she had learned from her grandmother. *If you didn't need to feel welcome, how could you be made to feel unwelcome?*

Reshma slipped her finger into the hook of Preethi's pinky as she marveled at how Narsa's cotton crops had blossomed into fluffy little clouds. She followed the rustle of Preethi's anklets to the kitchen and sank her face into her neck. They pressed their bodies together in a darkened afternoon room as Preethi's younger brother, Tarun, recited multiplication tables outside.

One evening, when Preethi complained about a pulled muscle in her leg, Reshma asked if she wanted a massage, and began kneading her calves. Preethi's father, Ushanna, who drank his tea silently in another corner of the room, watched Reshma's hands move in widening circles farther and farther up his daughter's legs. Preethi's face grew soft in a way that made him uncomfortable.

Ushanna cleared his throat. "You must have important work in Mumbai," he said. "Don't let us keep you from work."

"We are family," Reshma answered. "What's more important than family?"

As months went by, and the frequency and duration of Reshma's visits increased, Preethi's parents started to resent her for unsettling the peace of their home. Suddenly Preethi's conversation overflowed with foolish ideas about moving to the city for work. Reshma's name rolled off her tongue when she meant to call out to an aunt or a cousin. In Reshma's company, she looked at her parents with a wild look in her eyes, as if she had just remembered that they also lived there.

Preethi's father worried that his daughter was losing interest in her studies, putting the whole family in danger of losing the scholarship that covered the cost of meals when their crop failed. When he sat down to talk to her, he watched her eyes dreamily wander to the triangle of sunlight where Reshma squatted in a frothy rivulet, washing clothes as she sang to herself.

"Have you gone deaf?" Preethi's mother would explode at the defiance that blinked back in Preethi's eyes. When Preethi became so engrossed in Reshma's company, giggling at whatever inside joke was always brewing between them, Narsa's voice stopped reaching her.

The day before Bathukamma, the festival of flowers to celebrate the goddess of fertility during harvest season, Preethi insisted on taking Reshma to a shrine at the outskirts of the village, where she somehow always managed to find peace whenever her mind was in an upheaval. In the past weeks, Preethi told Reshma, she had felt herself vanish into feelings she could not explain, worrying about what the future held for them.

"I want this forever." Preethi reached for Reshma's hand. "That is the only way I will be at peace."

"We will be together forever," Reshma promised.

"Our relationship will become unbreakable only once it gets a name," she said. "We have to get married."

Reshma unhooked her gold locket and put it around Preethi's neck. "Mrs. Preethi Reshma Mokenwar," she announced. "My wife and my life."

That night, as Reshma and Preethi stretched out together in front of the television, entwining their bodies under a blanket, blushing at the fresh memory of their secret wedding, Narsa watched from a distance, drying pots and pans with the loose end of her sari and putting them down with an escalating violence. *What did Reshma want from them? Why was she refusing to go home? Why was she always stuck to Preethi? Why was Preethi always stuck to her?*

"Who will pay the rent here if she keeps running away from work?" Reshma's father, Babu, complained to Preethi's mother on the phone. "Her mother's hands have turned into jute from scrubbing dirty dishes. How long will my old bones sit in a driver's seat?"

"Preethi's studies are also suffering," Narsa said.

"What's really going on between them?" Babu asked.

The obviousness of the question suddenly plunged Narsa into an abyss of worry. After that, she could not rest. She stood in the kitchen, silently burning at the sight of Preethi's and Reshma's sleeping bodies. They were curled up facing each other, as if they had fallen asleep midsentence, and Reshma's hand rested loosely on Preethi's waist.

Narsa picked up a cooking pot and threw it to the floor. Reshma sat up with a start and sleepily watched Narsa drag Preethi's whimpering body to a mat in her corner of the room. Hours later, when Ushanna's snores had turned into long hisses, Narsa sensed Preethi crawl out and climb into Reshma's sleeping mat again.

The next day, when Reshma sat down to braid Preethi's hair while she arranged wild flowers in the shape of an ancient temple dome for the harvest festival, Narsa threw Reshma's bags outside the door and told her to never come back.

Chapter 6

You Look to Me, I Look to You

After Reshma Mokenwar was asked to leave and the blanket of wilting flowers from the harvest festival was swept aside, a mournful silence fell over the Sarikela household. To Narsa, it was the sound of shame at whatever perversity had been going on between her daughter and "the divorcée from the city." To Ushanna, it was the sound of a fragile peace that was shattered every now and then by the shriek of his daughter's ringing phone and the echo of cries that followed it.

To Preethi, it was the pop of a bubble bursting. The pain of enforced separation from Reshma had brought back memories of the worst day of her life nine years ago, in 2008, when the sky was clear, the earth was parched, and the air was thick with smoke rising from a cotton-ginning factory. Preethi saw herself as a nine-year-old, wearing a blue frock that reached her ankles, hair swept into two limp plaits woven with red ribbons, puttering behind her fifteen-year-old sister, Pooja, on the way to school. When Pooja collapsed suddenly in a river of sewage on the way to the exam, Preethi thought her sister's body had temporarily revolted from worrying too much about grades.

But as Pooja's eyeballs rolled up into her sockets, her body stiffened like it had turned into wood, and a cloud of foam covered her mouth, Preethi felt herself turn to ice. She collected the sounds around her and heard a succession of heavy footsteps descending into the river of sewage that sucked at her sister's body. She heard screeching brakes, blaring horns, and shouts of their father's name. Suddenly everything jumbled into a diabolical force, and she heard nothing but the siren of an ambulance as she watched her sister's body be flopped onto a stretcher. Pooja's arms and legs were tossed to the side, her face was slick with sweat, her plaits and their red ribbons were stiffened with muck.

At the funeral, murmurs that an empty bottle of insecticide had rolled out of Pooja's schoolbag rose thick with the smoke from her pyre. Neighbors and relatives said the suicide had been the result of a doomed love affair. The shame of being pregnant and unmarried, they said, had forced Pooja to kill herself. That day, Preethi learned that love could be a cause of death, like an accident or disease. As she returned to go through life, she carried the weight of that realization deep in her bones.

After Pooja's last rites, no one from the Sarikela family left the house except to go to school or work. For years, Preethi's ears rang with the deafening siren of a phantom ambulance that carried away the remains of her sister. Whenever she sat down to plait her hair with red ribbons, her fingers felt sticky, as if they were covered with the muck that devoured her sister. It confused her when heroines did not die at the end of romantic movies.

As years passed, Preethi grew to resent her dead sister. She came to believe that Pooja's death had sentenced her parents to a shame that never left them. She saw it in her father's hunched shoulders, and she heard it in her mother's hurried footsteps. Preethi worked day and night to become the best student in her class so that she could replace their shame with pride, but she could never bring her parents back from the spectral grip of her sister's death. Preethi made a habit of scribbling "My family my life" on the last page of her notebook to remind herself of her duty.

◆——◇——➤

When Preethi finished high school, and her classmates started pairing off with boys from a nearby college, she started talking to a cross-cousin named Shekar Gadapa. He bought her stuffed animals with his salary from working part-time at a petrol pump, and she inquired periodically if he had eaten his meals. The boy was not the problem; she was looking for a feeling that never came. After months of sleepwalking through a relationship with Shekar, she suspected her sister's suicide had rendered her incapable of experiencing true love. Then she met Reshma, and within days of meeting her, Preethi felt as if her heart had been gently cracked open and laid out in the sun. It was the first time in her life that she had experienced living for herself.

"If we can't live together," Preethi whispered into the phone to Reshma in the days after her parents asked the older woman to leave, "let's die together."

"Until we have to die, why don't we give life a chance and run away somewhere far away?" Reshma said.

"Where will we go?"

"Wherever we can be together."

"Where will we sleep, and what will we eat?"

"We will work," Reshma said. "I have some money."

On the morning of October 5, 2017, five months after they fell in love, when Preethi's father was at work at the village irrigation department, her mother was out working in the field, and her brother was in school, Preethi took a bus to the city of Adilabad and met Reshma at the railway station. They boarded the first train leaving the village and allowed their tired bodies to be lulled into a contorted sleep in an empty seat by the window.

◄┄┄◊┄┄►

After midnight, Preethi's eyes opened suddenly as the train pulled into Manmad, a village deep in the state of Maharashtra, three hundred miles from home. Even in the desolation of the night, the place felt familiar, filling her with the sense that she had seen the turmeric yellow arches of the terminal building and walked on the tar-coated platform before. Slowly, a faint memory of standing on the overpass as a young girl, counting shadows near the tracks during a family pilgrimage years earlier, startled her awake. She shook Reshma to tell her that this station was near Shirdi, the town where the spiritual leader Sai Baba was known to have once lived as a homeless man.

"Sai Baba is giving us a sign," Reshma announced with a wistful smile. "We will be safe here." She shuffled behind drowsily as Preethi stepped off the train and walked to the ticket counter in a trance to ask about buses leaving for Shirdi, dazzled by the good fortune that had delivered them to the Baba's abode.

The temple complex, where the mortal remains of Sai Baba, who died in 1918, were buried in a chamber made from white marble and gold, was ringed by a melee of markets selling pocket idols of the saint, wind-up toys that spouted his inspirational quotes, robes, scarves, video games about his life, books, stickers, and flowers. Even before sunrise, the market roads were bustling.

Reshma and Preethi waded through throngs of pilgrims and joined a line of damp bodies inching in the direction of the shrine. Preethi fanned her neck with a folded handkerchief, and Reshma enveloped her in a fierce embrace to ward off the stray hands that brushed women's breasts and snapped the elastic of their underwear in the anonymity of exactly these kinds of crowds. At one point, a festive murmur rippled through the devotees that a lamp had magically flickered to life inside the temple. Preethi decided Sai Baba had beckoned them to his town to bless their new life together.

When the gates opened for sunrise prayer, the crowd surged toward the temple. They were squeezed into metal dividers and forced into orderly queues to prepare for an assembly-line viewing of the shrine of the spiritual master. Reshma and Preethi were pushed along into a whirlwind of incense and light: toward the marble idol of Sai Baba seated on a gold throne adorned with gemstones, standing before it, beyond it, and back out into daylight.

Of the five hundred rupees ($7) Reshma had saved from her salary after contributing to bills at home, they had already spent two hundred fifty ($3.50) on train and bus tickets to Shirdi. "Don't worry," Reshma said to Preethi, equally determined to wring a higher truth from landing in the temple town. "Sai Baba will show us the way."

They wandered the town until they arrived at a row of identical low-rise buildings interspersed with trees whose canopies were tightly pruned to look like parasols. A small crowd milled near a wobbly table where a clerk distributed registration forms for subsidized accommodations for the poor. For two nights at the ashram, the clerk said, they would have to pay two hundred rupees ($2.50). That would leave them with only fifty rupees (60 cents), the cost of a plate of idlis.

Sai Baba had guided them to a safe house, but the rest of the work had to be done by them. Reshma took the clerk aside, and suddenly she fell to his feet, beating her chest and calling him a messenger of Sai Baba, the only man on earth who could save them with his generosity. She said that they were destitute sisters looking to start a new life. Preethi, burning with shame, stood at a distance, watching Reshma conduct a conversation with the clerk's slippers. When a crowd started to form, the clerk agreed to waive the charges, desperate to end the embarrassment.

That night, long after everyone in the hall had drifted off to sleep, Preethi still tossed and turned, unable to put the day's events out of her mind. She studied a poster of a close-up of Sai Baba's eyes and tried to make sense of the message inscribed beneath it: "You Look to Me, I Look to You." If Preethi saw a complete version of herself in Reshma and Reshma saw herself in Preethi, did it matter what others saw in them? Would Reshma and Preethi have to pretend to be sisters their whole lives? If they had left their homes to be their true selves, why were they forced to weave a new web of lies? If their world was too big for their small village, were they too small for the big world?

Suddenly Preethi ached for her parents. She did not want to talk to them; she only wanted to be comforted by the sound of their breathing, so she took Reshma's phone and dialed her father from under the covers.

⟵⋯◇⋯⟶

In 1860, British lawmakers, likely in tailcoats, cocked hats, and lace cuffs, drafted Section 377 of the Indian Penal Code criminalizing "carnal intercourse against the order of nature," to protect their men from "getting corrupted in colonies with morally lax norms." Section 377, modeled along King Henry VIII's Buggery Act of 1533, conflated homosexuality with bestiality and pedophilia, making these crimes punishable with ten years in prison. After the British left India in 1947, the law lingered behind like an accidental gift of colonialism, like tea and cricket.

The ultimate ambition of the colonized, the revolutionary French West Indian theorist Frantz Fanon wrote in his 1961 book, *The Wretched of the Earth*, is to resemble the colonizer to the point of disappearing in him: "The look that the native turns on the settler's town is a look of lust, a look of envy; it expresses his dreams of possession—all manner of possession."

Over centuries of colonial rule, Indians internalized homophobia as a precious marker of modernity, exposing our own dreams of possession. We confused homophobia with Indianness, even though our mythology brimmed with references to homosexuality, and our religious texts preached the idea of a genderless soul and marriage as a union of two souls. Hindu scriptures spoke of gods making love outside the confines of marriage and spirits flowing in and out of gendered bodies, but the contents of religious texts and the social life of religious practice operate in vastly separate realms.

Within the confines of the family structure, same-sex love is treated like a dirty secret. Often it is seen as a half-truth protected fiercely inside a fortress of denial until it can be totally erased through a heteronormative marriage.

On the way to the ashram one afternoon, Preethi told Reshma about two girls from her village who disappeared together. Months later, she heard that the girls were found and handed over to a healer who specialized in black magic and hypnotism.

"No one knows what he did to the girls in that room," Preethi said. "But when they went back home to their families, they both agreed to marry whomever their parents chose for them."

"If some mother-prick sister-prick tries to separate us," Reshma fumed, "I'll tear his limbs, break his bones, crush his head."

One scorching afternoon, when the whole town of Shirdi felt like it had been set on fire as a prelude to a Sai Baba miracle, Reshma and Preethi waited at the gate of a luxury hotel to catch the breeze of air-conditioning escaping from sliding glass doors. Preethi occasionally complained that her head spun, and Reshma handed her a bottle of water to remind her that they had only thirty rupees (40 cents) left. By evening, when Preethi's grumbles had turned into a bitter silence, they stumbled into a budget teahouse in the temple market.

The restaurant, a dim room with chocolate-brown walls, was crammed full of plastic tables covered in the spills of previous meals. A large woman with the face of a Russian nesting doll lorded over the teahouse from the cashier's counter under a poster of Sai Baba with his hand raised in a transcendent farewell. She totaled bills and changed cash with a quiver of her lower lip, kept an eye on the window where her cooks sweated in a circle of fires, barked orders across the room, and bestowed the smallest of smiles to friendly customers.

Preethi felt the woman's biting gaze on her body as she watched them slink into plastic chairs in a distant corner of the teahouse, lean across the table to conspiratorially run their eyes down the menu's price column, and order only a single plate of dosa for sharing. But once the meal restored Preethi's spirits, she noticed that the woman gave orders in the Telugu dialect of her and Reshma's villages, a wonderful surprise in this part of Maharashtra.

"Even her curses sound like music to my ears," Preethi remarked. "Reminds me of home."

"So it's decided," Reshma said as she wolfed down the last mouthful. "We'll convince her to give us jobs in this hotel and settle down in Shirdi." Three weeks had passed since they arrived in town, and since the ashram clerk's generosity had started to shrink, it had become necessary to think about a more permanent arrangement.

As Preethi watched Reshma walk over to the counter to strike up a conversation with the grumpy cashier in their mother tongue, she shook with silent laughter. This is what Preethi loved about Reshma. She could take an impossibility and turn it into an opportunity. She could make being stone broke and homeless feel like an adventure.

The next day, they sold Reshma's gold chain for ten thousand rupees ($159) to put down the deposit on a room on the roof near the temple. It was small, with green walls, a tin roof, a window with shutters made of cardboard, and a mud floor covered partly in broken tiles. Reshma looked around warily, masking her relief at finding a place within their budget with a grand show of displeasure so that the landlady would not be tempted to increase the rent. Preethi took in the room slowly, like someone touring an exhibition of rare and precious treasures. She tapped a wall and pressed her ear against it in a mixture of excitement and fear, as though she were waiting to hear a heartbeat. She took long strides along the length and breadth of the house as though she were measuring it to see if it fit her dreams. "Plates, bowls, cups, spoons, pots, and a pan," she muttered to herself to make a mental note of the things they would have to buy.

Preethi and Reshma would start their lives together inside this house. It would look like every house they had ever lived in, but it would be the only place in the world that would be *theirs*. They would work in the hotel as wait staff and live in this room as a married couple. Within these beautiful, crumbling walls, they would preserve the freedom and dignity of their love. They would live out their dreams, running their hands over each other's waist whenever they pleased, feeling alive and awake in each other's company. The house would always be fragrant with the smell of fresh ginger, cardamom, and incense. It would reverberate with Sai Baba's devotional songs. Within these walls, no one could force them to pretend to be sisters.

That afternoon, in one of the markets by the temple, as Preethi bent down to inspect an array of secondhand pots displayed on a towel on the footpath, she felt a shadow lurking behind her. When she turned to look, it had vanished. Hours later at home, while she was arranging a constellation of plastic bottles containing hair oil, tooth powder, talcum powder, and shampoo on an upturned cardboard box, she heard a knock on the door.

"So, sister?" Two men from her village stood at the door. "Do we look familiar?"

This was exactly how Preethi had feared this would end; the way countless romantic tracks pivoted into tragedies in her favorite Telugu serials. Men with small smiles and big misconceptions about their place in the world barged into the lives of happy couples and stood in their living rooms, surveying it with authority, breathing in the fragrance of their ginger and cardamom, contemplating whether to regard the runaways with amusement or pity.

"No?" Reshma pushed Preethi aside and blocked the door. "Who are you looking for?" Reshma had never seen these men before, but Preethi knew them from the smell of her village. The older man with the large forehead and a velvety mustache was Limbadri Baba, who was neither a village chief nor a police officer but a figure who commanded respect for his work resolving family disputes. The younger man was a sidekick.

"We'll get to know each other on the way to the village," Baba said. "Your parents have filed missing person complaints."

Limbadri Baba helped himself to the folding chair and explained how he had reached them. Preethi's father, Ushanna, had received a call from an unknown number late one night and sensed his daughter's silent sniffles. He had forwarded the number to Reshma's father, Babu, who had reached out to Limbadri Baba and requested him to use his contacts with the police to trace their location. For days, the men had been roaming the temple markets of Shirdi, showing photos of Reshma and Preethi to passersby and shopkeepers, until they finally stumbled into a pharmacy owned by their new landlady's brother-in-law.

Preethi's skin turned cold, and her cheeks reddened. Barely a month had passed since they had started their life together, and she had jeopardized everything in a moment of vulnerability by calling home.

She turned to Reshma, still looking for the words to explain herself, when the landlady burst into the room, her sari brushing against the kitchen countertop and shattering a half-full glass of tea. She hurried Reshma and Preethi outside, throwing their things into blue plastic bags, dragging their slippers to their feet, promising to keep the room exactly how they were leaving it until they came back. For now, though, she was desperate for them to leave, before the commotion drew a crowd and invited a police and municipality inspection.

As they climbed into Baba's car, Reshma secretly slipped Preethi a piece of the splintered teacup and said, "If we can't live together—"

Preethi finished the thought: "Then we'll die together."

PART TWO

Neetu Rani and Dawinder Singh, young lovers from a village in the northern Indian state of Haryana, elope to New Delhi to take shelter with the Love Commandos, a group of vigilantes who protect couples marked for honor killings by their families. Neetu is a Hindu of the Panchal caste, and Dawinder is a Sikh from the Mehra caste. They come from a place where councils of unelected elders enforce the caste system and punish intermarriage.

Chapter 7

Dirty Children

O ne winter afternoon in January 2017, Sanjoy Sachdev, the chairman of the Love Commandos, coordinated a rescue mission from his bed for the benefit of a foreign journalist who wanted to make a documentary film about his work. The daughter of a government official in Bareilly, a town in the northern state of Uttar Pradesh, had been kidnapped by her relatives while returning home from work in the New Delhi suburb where she lived with her husband, who was from a lower caste. Sachdev, horizontal and smoking a cigarette, reached his police contacts and tweeted at state officials.

"Love Commandos," he said into the phone.

"Yes, speaking," he continued.

"Yes, yes, the girl has been taken for statement?"

"I see."

He turned to the journalist who was sitting in a cane chair beside his bed. "That was the superintendent of the Bareilly police," he said. "The couple has not left yet because there is one more hurdle." Since local elections had been announced, and the police were not allowed to leave the district without permission from the election commission, Sachdev explained, a private car needed to be arranged to bring the couple to safety.

"The car will cost five thousand rupees to go and come. Plus toll, driver's stay, and food," he said into the phone before turning to the journalist with a sad face. "We have sold everything for India's love couples, but it is just not enough."

Neetu and Dawinder stood mast straight in the doorway with serious faces and waited their turn. Whenever a prospective donor visited the shelter, Sachdev described his lofty ideals about freedom and choice, asked the runaways to talk about how the Commandos had saved their lives, and shared a pressing life-or-death situation that could be solved with a donation from whoever was sitting in the cane chair. He did not like the runaways to say too much, so they were counted on to interpret the twitches of his eyebrow as a cue to stop talking. In the month since Neetu and Dawinder had been in the shelter, they had participated in the exercise so many times, they knew what to expect.

Sachdev would explain at great length that the Commandos were protecting couples in seven secret shelters in New Delhi and a network of hundreds of others across the country, but he refused to divulge any more details, saying it would compromise his clients' safety. He would say the group's rescue work had impressed chief ministers and police chiefs, who showed their support by fast-tracking help to cases flagged by the Commandos. He would hold up a tattered folder of press clippings and boast that thousands of articles in hundreds of languages had been written about the Commandos. He would talk about the numerous invitations to appear on television shows and at film screenings that they had turned down to focus on the real work of building a progressive country from the ground up. Within a year, he would say, they planned to expand the Love Commandos into Pakistan and Bangladesh.

The only obstacle, Sachdev would say with a long sigh, was finances. The Commandos needed at least a million rupees ($15,000) every month to keep the shelters running. For the shelter in New Delhi, they paid twenty-six thousand rupees ($400) in monthly rent. He also had to cover the electricity, water, and grocery bills for the fifteen or so people who lived there at any given time. "Multiply that by eight for the secret shelters," he would say, then pause for dramatic effect. "We need help because, as you know, this is a very big mission."

Sometimes marriages needed to be registered at short notice, Sachdev went on, which required a government fee of another ten thousand rupees ($150). Then there were couples who could not afford their own wedding ceremonies, which meant covering expenses for ghee, sandalwood, the priest's tip, garlands, and sweets. Some couples needed to be rescued; that called for cars, walkie-talkies, and emergency funds. Photocopying and notarizing documents cost money. And even though the Love Commandos operated within the law, gifts had to be sent during the festivals of Diwali and Eid to "speed up" officials they relied on for help. It was true that the retired tennis star Björn Borg and the matchmaking service Shaadi .com had both pledged donations as part of their corporate social responsibility efforts, but the Commandos got by primarily from the generosity of visitors who came to their shelter and saw for themselves the destitution of India's young lovers.

"Let me see if I can arrange money for the car," he spoke into another phone. "A very kind journalist is sitting in front of me right now."

As Sachdev steered his pants around his waist and walked the journalist to her car, the couples gathered on the balcony to see whether he had managed to convince her to part with a donation.

"He fleeces us and he fleeces them," one of the women muttered. "But where does all the money go?"

The next morning, Kajal and Ridhipatisidhi, the couple from Bareilly, arrived at the shelter. Ridhipatisidhi, who worked at a multinational company, sank into his chair as Sachdev told the story of Lord Shiva and Mother Parvati's intercaste marriage. Kajal, who wore a stylish roll-neck sweater and dangling gold earrings, wept as she looked around. Immediately, Sachdev inspected their papers, which included a religious certificate but not a court-issued license, so he got right down to starting their legal registration.

Neetu and Dawinder had been in the shelter for several weeks, but Sachdev had still not taken their paperwork to the marriage registrar. Whenever they asked, he received mysterious calls informing him the registrar office was closed. He stuck his head out the balcony and declared there was too much traffic. Sometimes he claimed an aunt or uncle had died in his village, and he went into silent mourning. Other times his back started to pain him or his blood sugar rose. Sachdev asked them to be patient until the shortage of funds was taken care of, but everyone knew that money was a perennial problem at the shelter. When Neetu reminded him that marriage registration cost only a few hundred rupees, and they had paid close to fifty thousand already, Sachdev looked hurt and said he had treated them like his own children, but she was bringing money between them.

"No need to call me Baba, since I am no one to you," he would say bitterly. "You may call me Sir."

After the Bareilly couple's registration was taken care of, the other couples started to grow anxious about what was holding up their paperwork.

"Whatever they wanted to do for us, they have already done," said Bhavika, the young wife from Gujarat, a state on India's western coast. "They want to keep us here forever so they can keep showing us to donors and taking money in our name."

"Every day there is a new excuse to delay our paperwork," Neetu complained.

"The Bareilly couple look wealthy," Sanjay, Bhavika's husband, observed.

"We are also from good families, and we have also paid in thousands," Bhavika said. "Why should we sit here and get taken for a ride?"

Lately, it seemed that Sachdev had sensed the stillness of a brewing rebellion. Suddenly he would barge into the couples' room, turn off the TV, and announce that he was saddened to witness India's youth squandering its future. If the neighborhood temple distributed free food on a holy occasion, he would declare the shelter kitchen closed and instruct the couples to line up outside the gate like the hungry and homeless people they really were. If the couples did not go downstairs in time to play cricket with a commando's young son, he would threaten to beat them. "Is your last name Mehra or Behra?"—*deaf* in Hindi—Sachdev would shout when Dawinder was slow to respond. "Do you have ears that can do the job of listening, or are they just for show?"

The day Kajal and Ridhipatisidhi came, Dawinder shouted at Neetu for eating sweets the newcomers had brought. Neetu removed her *choora* in a fit of rage and threw the bangles to the ground. Later, she confided to her dairy: "Dav said that he will drop me to my house tomorrow. Those words pricked me like a needle. But I consoled my heart and went to sleep. Till four in the morning, Dav was trying to talk to me. I said, okay, I will forgive him. Today I forgave him for the twenty-fifth time. Now I have to stop keeping count."

Moonlight poured into the bedroom from the street through a small window. Everyone appeared to be asleep, but then Neetu noticed a couple rocking under a mountain of quilts. She knew how elusive privacy was at the shelter, but she could not keep herself from laughing. Dawinder, rousing at the sound of her voice, looked up and sank his head into the pillow, laughing too.

Early one morning, when Dawinder took the shelter's dog, Romeo, for a walk, he stopped at the ATM so that he could buy Neetu a cake for their first-kiss anniversary. To his shock, he discovered that his savings account had been wiped out. Dawinder thought it would be disrespectful to ask Sachdev point-blank where his money had disappeared after he had shared his PIN, so he asked to borrow money for shampoo instead. He hoped Sachdev would understand what he was really asking and would provide a convincing explanation for how his money was used. "Take it tomorrow," Sachdev said instead. "Will your wife become less beautiful if she does not have a bath today?"

Sachdev had grown impatient with Dawinder after he had turned down the suggestion to take a waiter's job in a hotel down the street. Sachdev wanted Dawinder to settle down in New Delhi and live in the shelter for free in exchange for helping out. But he could not be persuaded to stay even with the offer of an additional commission for standing in as a witness for the temple weddings of new runaway couples, running errands to the registrar office, replacing broken bulbs and knobs at the shelter, and bringing Sachdev his morning tea.

"Why do you want to go back to Haryana and die?" Sachdev asked him one evening.

"Baba, my mummy and daddy are waiting for me," Dawinder said as he massaged the older man's feet. "When will our registration be done?"

"Look at you talking back!" Sachdev swung his legs off the bed in disgust. "We were your family when your family left you."

After the Bareilly couple's registration, Dawinder could no longer bring himself to think of Sachdev's bad temper as an endearing eccentricity. For the first time since they arrived at the shelter, he started to feel that some wrong had been done to him. Late one night, while lying in bed and waiting for sleep to come, Neetu brushed her hand against his neck. "Please leave me alone," he said with a force that felt like violence. "Don't talk to me." Neetu rolled over and told herself that fear was forcing Dawinder to be cruel. Hours later, as the sun rose over a landscape of tin roofs, Dawinder turned to Neetu's sleeping figure and hugged her.

"You told me to leave you alone," she said sleepily. "Why is your heart beating so fast?"

"Let's go home," he said. "I don't like it here anymore."

In mid-January, Sanjay and Bhavika, the couple from Gujarat, discovered they were pregnant. Sachdev decided that the Commandos could not risk being burdened by the cost of doctor's visits and newborn care, so he forbade all couples from sleeping together in the same room. "If I see any couple together in a room, I will myself lay down between them," Sachdev's voice boomed across the shelter. "Is that understood?"

On their first night apart, Neetu dreamed that Dawinder was stabbed in his stomach. After the second night, she woke up thinking that her husband had left her to go back to his parents. The sadness that overwhelmed her in her dreams turned into a hum of anxiety that followed her as she cooked, cleaned, watched TV. The minute Dawinder left her sight, the sorrow of the nights leapt up to her throat.

Early one morning, Dawinder disappeared into the neighboring building. Whenever Harsh Malhotra, the chief coordinator, who lived across the street with his wife and children, rang a bell from his window, the boys of the shelter were required to gather on the balcony to receive instructions to sweep, mop, walk the dog, or go out to buy a pack of cigarettes and a bottle of whisky. Malhotra wore rings with healing crystals to keep his bursts of anger in check, but his repertoire of curses remained so creative and scathing that even Sachdev acquired a nervous intensity around him.

That afternoon, Malhotra wanted Dawinder to press on his legs and keep him company watching TV. At lunchtime, when the other couples sat down to eat, Neetu refused to get out of bed. At teatime, she let her milky tea turn cold. By the time Dawinder was allowed to go late that evening, Neetu's irritation had turned into a bitter rage.

"It has become your habit to be upset," Dawinder told her. "You should have eaten something."

"And it has become your habit to listen to everyone but me," Neetu retorted. "I told you not to leave me. I told you I won't eat without you."

"What can I do if Harsh Papa called me?" Dawinder said. "You know I cannot leave until he dismisses me. What do you want from me?"

Neetu covered her face with a blanket to hide her tears because she suddenly felt foolish. Dawinder sat by her bed as if a terrible exhaustion had drained away his will to argue. The pressure cooker whistled in the kitchen. Water from a tap came in coughs. Steel plates and spoons clanked. A voice called out for Neetu to roll rotis, and Dawinder lifted the blanket from Neetu's face and gazed into her eyes. "Look at what we have become," he said. "Before getting us married, these Love Commandos will get us divorced."

◆━━━◆━━━◆

By late January 2017, two months after Neetu and Dawinder arrived, the shelter started to empty out. By some miracle, the families of Afsana and Malkit, the Muslim-Sikh couple from Delhi, grew tired of the hostility and decided to take them back. Ridhipatisidhi and Kajal, the Bareilly couple, moved out and returned to their well-paying jobs. When Bhavika and Sanjay declared that they wanted to leave for Gujarat, Sachdev sent their IDs and documents to Malhotra for safekeeping across the street to keep the couple from running off at night. Without valid IDs, registration would never be possible, and they would risk being separated.

"Only Neetu is my good daughter because she doesn't fight with me," Sachdev said one afternoon, flapping his thighs. "She will bring me tea every morning from tomorrow."

Hearing Sachdev talk about them as if they were destined to be permanent fixtures at the shelter, Dawinder felt a shock of urgency. If they ended up being the last couple at the shelter, they might never be able to get out.

That afternoon, Dawinder secretly scanned their IDs and documents to Sachdev's computer and emailed them to himself when the older man stepped out to go to the bank. The only thing he could not find was the paper that contained their username and password, without which it would be impossible to complete their marriage registration. He worried that if he asked Sachdev where the paper was or if Sachdev sensed that they wanted to leave, he would send all their documents over to Malhotra, as he had done with Bhavika and Sanjay. "Fast, fast, fast," Neetu muttered as she kept watch. "Even the walls have eyes and ears in this shelter."

One winter morning, eight weeks into the shelter, Dawinder took Romeo the dog for a walk and made a surreptitious call to his cousin Shanty Singh, who had driven the getaway car. The cousin told him that back in Kakheri, his parents' lives had been upended. They were shuttling from one relative's home to another, fearing violence from Neetu's family. Hearing this, Dawinder decided that they would leave the shelter that very afternoon.

"Mummy and Daddy are wandering from here to there. They have not gone home since we left. I have never given them any happiness. Daddy has never worn good clothes or eaten good food. Mummy's legs don't work properly." Dawinder pressed his wrists into his eyes to stop the tears from falling out.

"We are dirty children," Neetu said mournfully as she rested her head on his shoulder.

When Neetu and Dawinder started to pack their bags, Sachdev hovered around them. He said he had become so attached to them that he could no longer do without them. Couldn't they stay a little bit longer for the sake of their old Baba? He reminded them about the couples who had left the shelter to be with their families, only to become victims of honor killings.

"Please understand, children, it is not safe," he said. "Why do you want to go and get killed?"

When it became clear that they had made up their minds to leave, Malhotra burst into the shelter and declared that he would not hand over their IDs and documents. He refused to give them the username and password to complete the marriage registration. Without any evidence, they were as good as unmarried.

"Call your father," Malhotra demanded.

"Why?" Dawinder said.

"It's our policy," he said.

"You didn't want to talk to them when we came here," Dawinder said. "Why do you want to talk now?"

"Look who has a big tongue inside his mouth." Malhotra's face shone with sweat. "Talk back once again," he threatened, "and watch me call the girl's father."

Malhotra threw their tattered bags in the dust, and Sachdev knelt down to check for stolen items. "Are you sure this is yours?"

Sachdev held up a new shirt with an impish smile. "It will look better on me." Neetu grabbed it, stuffed it back into the bag and demanded the cell phones they had handed over when they arrived.

Sachdev returned only two of their three phones and kept the expensive one pressed under an elbow. "Go, run," he told them. "You're not getting this one." Neetu pried the last phone from his grip and slammed the door behind them.

Chapter 8

Manoj and Babli

On June 23, 2007, a team of forensic doctors at the government medical college in Rohtak, one of the largest cities in the northern Indian state of Haryana, received two dead bodies for examination. One corpse, a nineteen-year-old woman, had been recovered from a canal near the village of Sandlana. The other, that of a twenty-three-year-old man, was found ten miles downstream in a village called Kheri Chopta. Both bodies were bloated and had been decomposing inside tattered gunnysacks for more than a week.

In their report, the doctors wrote that the woman's body was covered in maggots. The legs and hands were tied with a rope. Fingers and toes were missing. There was no neck.

The man's face was disfigured. There was a plastic rope around the neck. The loose ends of the rope were tied around the feet. The eyes, ears, and mouth were deformed. The genitals had been disfigured.

The doctors sealed part of the woman's silver anklet and a scrap of the man's shirt in plastic bags and handed over the bodies to the police to cremate as unclaimed destitutes. A week later, they were identified as Manoj and Babli Banwala from Karora, a village an hour's drive from Neetu's and Dawinder's Kakheri.

◆┄┄◇┄┄▶

Two years earlier, Manoj and Babli met at an electric repairs shop in their village and fell stubbornly in love. Manoj, who had a mop of furious, thick hair and darting eyes, worked there as an apprentice. Babli, who had a swinging plait and a smiling face that often conveyed a hint of boredom, belonged to an influential family of landowners. They were both Banwala Jats by caste and shared the same *gotra*, or clan, which traced them to a common ancestor. In the eyes of their community, even though they were not directly related, they were brother and sister.

When murmurs of their relationship began circulating, Babli's family fixed her wedding to a stranger after harvest season. Weeks before the harvest, Manoj and Babli eloped to Chandigarh, the state capital, and married in a temple. Manoj's family thought he was spending the night at the shop, and Babli's family thought she was asleep in her room.

In the days after their elopement, Manoj's mother tried to lodge a missing person report, but the police refused to register it. Instead, they booked her for conspiring with Manoj to kidnap Babli, as police feared a local politician and leader from the khap panchayat who came out in support of Babli's family.

Across the northern Indian countryside, villages continued to be run by khap panchayats that represented the interests of gotras. Khap panchayats upheld social customs, including the belief that men and women within the same gotra and the same village were brothers and sisters. The Banwala khap panchayat, the gotra to which both Manoj and Babli belonged, held power in roughly forty villages around Karora.

On June 15, two months after they eloped, Manoj and Babli appeared at the district court in Kaithal, a town thirty miles from their village, to attest that they were legally married and no kidnapping had taken place. They knew it was dangerous to go back, but it was the only way to convince the police to drop the false charges against his mother.

The couple had applied for police protection and were granted a police party to escort them back safely to Chandigarh. No one from Manoj's family attended the trial, so that Babli's family would not get to know that the couple was in the area. But to their surprise, Babli's brother, Suresh, and cousin Gurudev arrived at court at the exact time of their hearing.

Afterward, a team of five policemen initially planned to accompany the couple to a bus stand in the town of Pehowa, where they would catch a public transport bus bound for Chandigarh. But when the couple pleaded that Babli's uncles and cousins and the khap leader were following them in a car, a police department superior instructed two of the five officers to board the bus and ride with them. However, at Pipli, a town sixty miles from their destination, the officers abandoned them, declaring that they could not travel beyond the boundary of their jurisdiction.

Manoj and Babli scrambled onto another bus leaving for New Delhi, eighty-five miles to the southeast, in the hope that they would lose her relatives, but halfway there, just as the bus was about to pull into a toll plaza near the town of Karnal, a van swerved in front of it, forcing the driver to stop. Manoj and Babli were abducted, and they were never seen again.

◆━━•◆•━━▶

In the days after Manoj's and Babli's disappearance, Manoj's mother, Chandrapati, filed a case of kidnapping with the intention of murder against Babli's brothers, cousins, uncles, and the leader of the khap panchayat. She told the police that her son had called from the Pipli bus stand to inform her that the escort party had abandoned them and Babli's relatives were following them. That was the last time she would speak to Manoj.

When Chandrapati returned home to Karora after registering the police complaint, the village council decreed that Manoj's family would be punished with economic sanctions for bringing dishonor to the village by filing a police complaint against respectable members of the community. Anyone who talked to them or did any business with them would be fined twenty-five thousand rupees and risk being ostracized themselves.

"Marry a Muslim if you must, marry a Christian, marry an old man, marry a cripple. Marry whoever you want, but always marry outside the village," Chander Singh Dalal, a khap ideologue, told reporters when Manoj and Babli's disappearance started to make headlines. "Never marry in the same village and the same gotra."

"If a marriage takes place within the same gotra, the consequences are bound to be harsh," Panwanjit Barwal, a leader of the Banwala khap panchayat, said at the All India Jat Organization two weeks after Manoj's and Babli's bodies were found. "To the leftist organizations who are espousing their cause, I would like to ask them to marry their sons to their daughters."

When Manoj's mother and his sister Seema returned home after identifying a scrap of Manoj's pink shirt and a piece of Babli's anklet, a stench had lodged itself deep beneath their fingernails. The autopsy report said that Manoj had been strangulated to death, and Babli had been forced to drink pesticide. The stench in their fingers did not leave no matter how much they scrubbed and washed their hands.

Days later, when they brought the ashes of Manoj and Babli from the municipal cremation ground, no one in the village agreed to sell them the mud urns needed to perform their last rites.

◆━━━◇━━━➤

In March 2010, the Karnal District Court held five members of Babli's family—her brother, Suresh; two uncles, Rajinder and Baru Ram; two cousins, Satish and Gurudev—and the leader of the khap panchayat guilty for the double murder.

"This court has gone through sleepless nights and tried to place itself in the shoes of the offenders and think as to what might have prompted them to take such a step, but nothing seemed to justify the act of committing such a heinous crime," Judge Vani Gopal Sharma announced as she sentenced the five members of Babli's family to death and a leader of the Banwala khap panchayat to life imprisonment for the couple's kidnapping and culpable homicide.

For the first time in public memory, the law had collided with tradition. A wave of stunned anger surged through the countryside. More than forty khap panchayats in the area convened in a grand council meeting to discuss a mass demonstration seeking an amendment to the Hindu Marriage Act, the law that codified marriage laws between Hindus, to include a ban on marriages within the same gotra. An amendment to the law would deter young couples such as Manoj and Babli and absolve khap panchayats and families of the responsibility to safeguard traditions. At the meeting, a donation box went around to collect funds to hire a team of lawyers on behalf of Babli's relatives and the khap leader as the case prepared to go into appeal in the Punjab and Haryana High Court.

For most of that summer after the sentencing, the murder of Manoj and Babli dominated prime-time television debates. Manoj's sister Seema, appearing on a television program called *Big Fight—Modern India, Medieval Justice?* to debate the issue of honor killings, described the hardships imposed on her family. "On one hand, we were dealing with the grief of losing Manoj and Babli," she said. "On the other hand, we were facing difficulties from the boycott. No one could talk to us. The milkman stopped selling us milk. We could not get cattle fodder. The potter refused to sell us the urns to hold the ashes of Manoj and Babli. At a time when we needed empathy—"

Another participant, Om Prakash Dhankar, the president of an umbrella body of khap panchayats, interrupted her. "Daughter, are you sure it was a khap panchayat? Which khap was it that was in your village?"

Lawyers and women's activists came to Seema's defense, saying the khap leader's attempts to intimidate her publicly would not be tolerated. The argument escalated to the point that the TV studio lights had to be switched off in the middle of filming to get the audience to quiet down.

"The conflict is not really between the views of the khap panchayat and the views of these ladies," Brajinder Singh Mann, a farmer from Haryana, said once the program resumed. "The conflict is between the urban way of thinking and the rural way of thinking. And the rural people have a right to their way of thinking."

Kirti Singh, a lawyer in the Supreme Court of India, took a contrary view, stating, "We are a country which has a constitution that has given equal rights to people. It has given young girls and young boys the right to choose their partner. Any custom that goes against these human rights cannot be upheld. That is Indian law. That is international law. And that is humanitarian law."

◆----◇----◆

In the weeks after the Karnal Court verdict, a team of lawyers in New Delhi headed by Singh, the Supreme Court lawyer, drafted a bill called the Prevention of Crimes in the Name of Honor and Tradition specifically to tackle honor crimes.

Honor crimes were a violation of the fundamental rights to life, liberty, and dignity guaranteed by the Indian constitution, the bill argued. And since there was no law to specifically prosecute honor crimes, there was no way to cover the full gamut of related crimes, which often included harassment, intimidation, economic sanctions, and social boycotts.

In the absence of an honor crime law, the police often acted in collusion with disgraced families. "Because right now, what's happening is that the police don't act for the couple; instead, they act for the girl's family," Singh later told me. "Because they, themselves, come, I suppose, from a society and a way of thinking that believes there shouldn't be choice marriages, particularly in cases where it's an intercaste marriage."

The bill sought to shift the burden of proof to the accused— a reversal of the principles of criminal justice, as in the case with anti-dowry laws. Thus, the onus would lie on khap panchayats and families of the couple to establish they were not guilty of punishing intercaste marriage. One of its provisions stated that if a couple told a public servant they wanted to be together, the police could not file a complaint against them. That would counter a common revenge tactic in which families filed false cases of kidnapping, as in Manoj's case.

The proposed law also defined honor killings separately from murder and suggested doing away with the Special Marriage Act's thirty-day-notice period that usually enabled relatives to track down couples and force them into submission. "I have no idea which genius thought of it in the first place," Singh said. "Anyone can marry under the Special Marriage Act: two Hindus, two Muslims, a Hindu and a Muslim—anyone who wants to have a civil marriage. I believe the clause was introduced precisely so that if somebody wanted to object to the marriage, they would have the time to do so."

In August 2010 Singh delivered her draft legislation to the Law Commission of India, an executive body tasked with legal reform. For the bill to become law, it required input from representatives of every state and union territory, along with approval by three national ministries, before it could be presented to a standing committee, which would then consider it for parliamentary debate. After Bhupinder Singh Hooda, the chief minister of the state of Haryana, strongly objected to the bill in a letter to the home minister, arguing that shifting the burden of proof could do more harm than good, the matter was turned over to the Law Commission.

Two years later, in 2012, the Law Commission released its own version of the bill, called Prevention of Interference with the Freedom of Matrimonial Alliance, which sought to prohibit intervention in marriage by khap panchayats. The new version said that honor crimes could be prevented if khap meetings were criminalized, but it did not account for the roles of families and police officials. "This bill will never be a priority for the government," Ravi Kant, another Supreme Court lawyer, told me. "The government doesn't want to put its hand somewhere it can get stuck."

On March 11, 2011, a year after the lower court held all the accused guilty, the Punjab and Haryana High Court acquitted the khap leader and Babli's cousin Satish for lack of evidence. The high court judges commuted the death sentences of the other accused, including Babli's brother, cousin, and two uncles to life imprisonment.

In their verdict, the judges stated, "Even in the twenty-first century, such a shameful act of hollow honor killing is perpetrated in our society. We feel that it is really a slur on the fine fabric of the Indian society. But, unfortunately, in this case, there is no eye witness to the occurrence. The entire case of the prosecution depends on the circumstantial evidence. As we have rendered the verdict based on the circumstantial evidence, our conscience does not permit us to confirm the death sentence awarded to the accused."

The next morning, in her home in Karora, Manoj's mother, Chandrapati, read newspaper headlines in a funereal silence. Three months before the high court verdict, a man carrying a homemade pistol had stormed the police academy where Manoj's sister Seema was training to become a police constable and threatened to kill her. "Now that these men are out, how will we ever live in peace?" Chandrapati told reporters.

◆┄┄┄◇┄┄┄►

Even as Manoj's family worried about their safety, their fight for justice had set into motion a chain of events that would for the first time in Indian history challenge the might of khap panchayats. A month after the high court's verdict, on April 19, 2011, while hearing an honor killing case from the southern Indian state of Tamil Nadu, a bench of Supreme Court judges declared khap panchayats "illegal and unconstitutional" and ordered the states to stamp them out. They said that honor killings should be punished with death sentences. "This is necessary as a deterrent for such outrageous, uncivilized behavior," the Supreme Court bench said. "All persons who are planning to perpetrate 'honor' killings should know that the gallows await them."

After the Supreme Court verdict, eighty khap panchayats convened in another grand council in Jind, a town in Haryana, to discuss ways to file a petition to get the court to review its order.

As the honor crime bill languished in red tape, waiting for responses from representatives of states a decade after it was first introduced in the wake of Manoj's and Babli's murders, newspapers continued to be filled with stories of honor crimes. Khap panchayats continued to operate with impunity as extrajudicial bodies.

At last, in 2018 a three-judge bench of the Supreme Court, including Dipak Misra, the chief justice of India, issued a framework of comprehensive guidelines to punish honor killings as the gravest of offenses until an honor killing law came into force. The court ordered state governments to identify areas where honor killings have been reported, supervise the activities of khap panchayats, videotape meetings to establish criminality, and hold police officers accountable for providing protection to couples facing threats.

In the Supreme Court's words, "honour killing guillotines individual liberty, freedom of choice, and one's own perception of choice. It has to be sublimely borne in mind that when two adults consensually choose each other as life partners, it is a manifestation of their choice which is recognized under articles 19 and 21 of the constitution. The human rights of a daughter, brother, sister, or son are not mortgaged to the so-called or so-understood honor of the family or clan or the collective."

In Karora, as the acquitted men returned to the village, Manoj's younger brother and sister dropped out of college to study at home. Their mother stuffed a tattered bag with case files to take to the lawyer's office in New Delhi to begin the process of appealing the acquittal of her son's murderers in the Supreme Court.

Mohammad Arif Dosani and Monika Ingle, a Hindu-Muslim
couple from the western Indian town of Nagpur, spend time
together in a large group of college friends whose company
feels like looking into a carnival-mirror reflection of Indian
multiculturalism—Hindus mingle with Muslims, and lower
castes with upper castes.

When Monika discovers she is pregnant with Arif's child, and
it is too late for an abortion, the illusion shatters. In Nagpur, the
birthplace of political Hindu nationalism, daily life is shaped by
millennia-old Hindu-Muslim prejudices. "If Hindus are snakes,
Muslims are mongooses," Arif says. "We will always be enemies
by nature."

Chapter 9

Love Jihad

After they left home the morning of August 29, 2017, Arif and Monika rode around in frantic circles for a while, a duffle bag pressed between them, waiting for instructions from their lawyer, Vilas Dongre, until they arrived at an ancient lake in the middle of Nagpur.

In the nineteenth century, a Muslim ruler commissioned the lake to supply water to the city and gave it an Urdu name. When a succession of Hindu kings arrived, they called it by a Sanskrit name. After independence from Great Britain, it turned into a tourist attraction named after Mohandas Gandhi. But at the turn of the new millennium, when the city administration began fishing out dead bodies from the water, it came to be known as Suicide Lake.

From the banks of the lake, the scattered city fit into a tight view, throwing its crowds, prejudices, possibilities, and arguments over the edge into a vast stillness. "Are you sure you don't want to turn back home?" Arif said to Monika. "You can tell your family you went to a friend's house, and we can stop this whole thing now."

"No," she muttered.

A busload of families arrived to go boating, and as they rambled to the bank, laughing and singing, they twisted their spines to see the crying faces of two strangers. Monika sobbed softly, throwing sideways glances at the tourists, and Arif slapped the tears off his cheeks.

They expected a call from Dongre within the hour. He would then take them to the local police station to hand over notarized copies of their marriage certificate and affidavits stating that they were adults who were leaving their homes to be together by choice. The police would inform Monika's parents, who would rush to take her home, but they would be in no position to legally separate the couple. By evening, Dongre had promised, they would be married, and their families would be exchanging sweets.

When the call came, though, their attorney's voice trembled. "Run away as fast as you can," he advised. Dongre had handed their papers to the police commissioner's assistant and become suddenly nervous about how Monika's family would process the news of their daughter's marrying a Muslim.

"Where, sir?" Arif asked. "We didn't bring clothes or money because you told us everything would be fine by evening." Arif had hoped the twenty-five thousand rupees ($350) he had paid Dongre after selling a mobile phone that cost twice as much would include a more dependable plan than standing orders to disappear.

"That you see," Dongre snapped. "But don't take a train, because they are bound to come looking at the railway station." The abrupt call restored the urgency to vanish, but beyond that, Arif's intelligence wilted. Monika, for her part, studied the water as if she were waiting for a great gust to carry them away. So Arif called his friend Akbar to ask what to do.

By the time the afternoon sun set, they had taken a bus to a nearby town and boarded a train to the countryside. The familiar views that comforted them had begun to disappear. Slowly, the city left them, then the trees lost their flowers. The rivers dried up, turning into barren sweeps, and Arif felt his throat turn coarse, as if he had swallowed a ball of hair. When the train pulled into Akola Junction, Monika leaned out to give herself a view of her destiny. What she saw was a great cloud of red dust.

As they watched the train disappear, leaving them in this wasteland of cinder, gravel, and thatched roofs, Arif sank to his haunches, and Monika dialed her sister. "Bhaga, listen," she said. "I've left with Arif." Bhagyashri screamed, begged, and howled. She warned Monika that Arif would betray her. She said their father had suffered a heart attack. She told her to hide somewhere and wait for her to get there. Their father was in the hospital. She promised to get her married to Arif. She said she would take them to the marriage registrar herself. Arif grabbed the phone before Monika grew weak, and he tossed the SIM card onto the tracks.

As dusk turned into night, and the platform emptied out as if to leave them to reflect on their life choices, Monika said she was hungry. Sitting across from her at a rickety table by the station, watching her study the menu with grave concentration, Arif burst out laughing. He found it hilarious that in the most serious situation of her life, she contemplated a plate of *poori bhaji*, potato curry and fried bread, over a bowl of idlis.

◆━━━◇━━━▶

Two hundred miles away in Nagpur, Vishal Punj was splayed on his couch, scrolling through WhatsApp, when he suddenly perked up, sensing a breakthrough in his political career. The nature of his work as chief convener of the Bajrang Dal's Nagpur Metropolitan chapter, the belligerent youth affiliate of the Sangh that has been described as a somewhat pathetic version of Adolf Hitler's thuggish Nazi Brownshirts of the 1930s, was unpredictable. It meant the drudgery of sweeping, mopping, and arranging chairs for a party meeting one day and the exhilaration of stopping traffic to perform a sword dance in honor of ancient Hindu warrior kings another.

Punj, an engineering graduate with an athletic build, a scraggly mustache, and a jovial face, had sunk a decade brushing aside income-generating work as a freelance road contractor to perform administrative tasks for the Bajrang Dal. Through the years, he had accumulated a Royal Enfield motorcycle, a collection of saffron shirts and scarves, and a slow-burning contempt for Muslims. Among friends, he was known as Bajrangi Paji Saheb, or Bajrangi Brother Sir, because his physical appearance demanded deference even as his personality induced affection.

What he had been waiting for was an exciting project that would display his full potential as a fearless soldier of the Hindu Nation.

That night, before leaving home to attend to the distress call on WhatsApp, he bowed to a constellation of deities in his living room, gliding from picture to picture, knowing that his time had finally arrived, even if his wife had responded to his enthusiasm with half-closed eyes and gone back to bed.

After midnight, Bajrangi Paji Saheb marshaled a swarm of motorbikes through the tin sheds of Hasanbagh until the deserted lanes narrowed to a row of cramped huts separated by a gap as wide as a pair of shoulders. Inside the shanty by an open sewer, Arif's aunt Akida drifted in and out of sleep, stretched out in front of the television, when she heard shouts outside. She turned to the TV in a daze to determine if the hero was in the middle of an action scene. But the shouts grew louder. Then she heard the short gate of her home clatter into a useless pile of rotted wood.

She shrieked and howled as a scrum of strangers broke into her house, stomping in with their big, dirty shoes, pushing their way in, banging doors, tearing down lines of wrung-out clothes, toppling over kitchen utensils. As she scanned the intruders, she fell silent the moment her gaze settled on the face of a girl who usually bumbled around her house, helping with chores, learning recipes, massaging her shoulders, relishing family stories. In the shadow of Bajrangi Paji Saheb's hulking presence, Monika's sister, Bhagyashri, looked like a stranger. Akida was stunned at the razor-sharp edge in her voice. The kind of language she used. The way she drew back her foot to kick a cooking pot in her path. How all her teeth became exposed when she yelled. The girl's face was as pale as a sheet, but her eyes were ablaze with *junoon*: a maddening vengeance.

"Bring them back!" she kept shouting. "Bring them back now! Bring them back right now!" The rest of Monika's family—her father and mother; her brother, Amit; and two aunts—watched quietly from the back.

Bajrangi Paji Saheb took Arif's uncle Rahim aside and asked how such a shameful crime had taken place under his watch. He spoke in a calm and leisurely way, not issuing threats, only inquiring as a well-wisher who wanted the best for both families. Rahim revealed everything he knew, which was nothing, since Arif had left home that morning without informing anyone.

A knot of neighbors gathered outside the home, and as the crowd parted to allow Bajrangi Paji Saheb's men to leave, Akida's twenty-year-old son, Jikar, ran out behind them. At a nearby pavement food stall, the men wound down with samosas and tea, discussing how to make an example of the Muslim family.

One of the men recognized Jikar from their day job at a factory. "Jikku," he asked, "was that your house? How could your brother take a girl from our community?"

"Brother, you tell me," the young man replied. "Does it not take two hands to clap?"

◆┄┄◇┄┄◆

The next morning, a swarm of Bajrang Dal men surrounded the Imamwada Police Station, seething and crackling like a flock of locusts. Bajrangi Paji Saheb emerged with Monika's brother, Amit, from the precinct house to a clamoring of "Jai Sri Ram"—"victory to Lord Ram"—when someone in the front said that the police were hesitant to file a case against the Muslim boy who had seduced and kidnapped a Hindu girl. As word trickled through the mob, shock turned into outrage, swelling into a tidal wave of fury, and someone lit a tire on fire and threw it at the police gate.

Across the country, since Prime Minister Narendra Modi and his Hindu nationalist Bharatiya Janata Party formed a government three years earlier in 2014, lynch mobs had begun popping up in towns and villages to punish the defilement of two sacred symbols: cows and women. Muslims were dragged out into the streets, beaten with hockey sticks, thrown to railway tracks, and struck with rocks.

The Imamwada Police, operating in a place primed for communal conflict, locked up its gates, summoned the antiriot squad, and
monitored the mob's temperament from a small window.

Later that morning, when the lawyer Vilas Dongre sent his in-
tern to the police station with copies of Arif and Monika's *nikah*
certificate and a letter stating that they were adults leaving by choice,
the mob hoisted the poor young man onto the hood of a parked
jeep and towered over him until they blotted out the sun. "Do you
understand what you people have done?" they shouted. "Do you understand the meaning of love jihad?"

At the time, Dongre was at home, sitting in front of his morning
tea, staring nervously at his blinking phone. Between midnight and
dawn, Bajrangi Paji Saheb had called every hour, asking where Arif
took Monika. He demanded to know where the lawyer lived, if he
was on the payroll of an Islamic terror outfit, and whether his bones
had ever been broken before.

As the afternoon sun sizzled, and the mob grew restless, the
station officer came out to promise in a weak voice that the police
would locate Arif and Monika within forty-eight hours. Bajrangi
Paji Saheb took out a handkerchief, wiped his face, and walked
away. It was time to pick up his daughter from school.

◆┄┄◇┄┄◆

Three days later, in Hasanbagh, children in twinkling long coats, or
sherwanis, flitted through narrow lanes, losing their slippers in small
rivers of blood that flowed from sacrificial animal slaughter for the
festival of Bakri Eid, the holiest day in the Islamic calendar. The
wealthiest families in the neighborhood tied up their goats to their
front door for display, fed and bathed them, and, on the day of cel-

ebration, yanked back their heads, slit their throats, and invited everyone to feast on mutton curry. The poorest families, like Akida's, waited to benefit from the rich's religious obligations of having to donate a third of the sacrificial meat.

The morning after the Bajrang Dal's ambush, Akida woke early and tried to pray, but her thoughts kept returning to the frightening events of the previous night. She wanted nothing more than to surrender the upheaval in her mind to her prayers, but Bhagyashri's voice continued to haunt her. "Bring them back!" Her voice sounded like hollow wood. "Bring them back now!"

Akida made tea, washed her face, and tried to pray again. When she finally clenched her eyes shut, bending down in prayer, Inspector Amol Jadhav of the Imamwada Police Station called for the third time that morning to ask if Arif had gotten in touch. She gave up and went to the kitchen to stir her anxiety into the pot of leftover meat that Jikar's boss had sent over for the festival. But as she began setting out plates, her son's phone rang.

"Yes, brother," she overheard him say. "Yes, I know where Arif is." Then his voice shook, and his new black shirt glistened with sweat. The police had traced Arif's phone to Akola Junction and rushed to a tin hut on the city's outskirts, where his sister Farheen lived with her husband, Zakir. They did not find Arif and Monika there, so they detained Zakir for questioning, shouting at him, throwing him in the dirt, and forcing him to call Jikar. Halfway through their conversation, a policeman snatched the phone and told Jikar that they were coming for him. In the background, the boy heard Zakir yelp.

The next minutes spun so fast that they scrambled into a blur. Jikar threw out his SIM card, put two shirts in a plastic bag, stuffed a thousand rupees ($13) in his pocket, and boarded the first bus leaving the city. At the bus station, Akida ran to a pavement stall to bring her hungry son a plate of samosas, but the bus was gone before she got back. As Akida watched Jikar disappear, knowing there was no way to reach him, the words that swirled in her head were *bhayanak manzar, bhayanak manzar*—crack of doom, crack of doom. By the time she reached home, two police cars were parked outside.

Hours later, Vilas Dongre finally answered his phone and advised Akida to rally people in Hasanbagh in case the elopement sparked a Hindu-Muslim riot. The lawyer's words eliminated the small comforts of the illusion that the worst had passed. She rambled through the neighborhood's crime-ridden streets half-crazed, blabbering everything to everyone. Someone advised her to fall at the feet of the clerics at the big mosque, but they turned her back, saying that their expertise was in religious matters and not political feuds. Someone else told her to ingratiate herself with a powerful local slumlord, who suggested carrying a bucket of kerosene in the presence of police officers so that they would believe her if she threatened to set herself on fire. In the end, Aunt Akida paid Dongre thirty-five thousand rupees ($473), a tattered bundle of small notes collected over a decade of cutting household expenses, to introduce her to a newspaper journalist and local politician, who promised to gather a crowd if her family came under attack.

At midnight, Akida rolled out her sleeping mat, but sleep did not come. Jikar was probably still hungry, wide awake on a railway bench somewhere, with his slippers tucked under his head. Whenever she closed her eyes, his face flashed and mutated in the darkness, so she tossed and turned until dawn broke. With the first whistle of the pressure cooker, Inspector Jadhav called to see if she knew anything new.

That afternoon, Akida was in her *namaaz*, chewing on the last verse of prayer, when she heard heavy footsteps approach. She opened her eyes to find the inspector standing behind her, his face on the verge of a sneer. She had wept thinking about the moment the police would come to take her since the day Arif left, but when it arrived, she felt no sense of crisis. When he said that she must report to the police station to provide an official statement and surrender her mobile phone for checking, she asked to see a warrant in a dull voice that lacked the desperation of her rehearsals. It was only when Jadhav advised her to shut up that a visceral fear reentered her body.

"You told me you are in Akola," she said to the inspector, with a wild look in her eyes. "Then how did you come here so fast?"

"I lied to you," he snapped. "Because you people never tell the truth."

As the police van carrying Akida dawdled through the slum's gloomy lanes, she memorized the faces of neighbors who gathered outside to relish the sight of her downfall. She saw the woman from two doors down clench a smile when policewomen threw Akida in the back of the van like she was a sack of dirty laundry. The butcher from down the lane fanned his stomach. The *maulana*, a cleric, muttered to himself at this unfolding of hell. Akida Khemani, a woman who had built a life of respect for her children from the scraps her husband spared, was reduced again to a snatch of neighborhood gossip.

Two hundred miles away in Basmath, Arif's father, Bashir, was curled up on the floor, kneading his wrists into his eyes, shaking hysterically whenever his phone rang. After Bajrangi Paji Saheb pressured the Imamwada Police into announcing that Arif and Monika would be located within forty-eight hours, Inspector Jadhav instructed Bashir to pick up his phone at the first ring. But the calls that came were from unknown numbers: a low voice threatening to set his house and shop on fire; a chuckle inquiring about the well-being of his youngest daughter, Shireen. At midnight, when the phone rang yet again, and Bashir began howling, Arif's mother, Tabssum, answered.

"If you don't tell me where my sister is," Bhagyashri screamed on the phone, "I will bury your whole family seven feet under!" Weeks earlier, when Tabssum visited Nagpur, Bhagyashri had driven her around the city on her scooter, showing Arif's mother wholesale cloth markets to source materials for her tailoring business. On that warm afternoon, the two of them had washed off the sun in the cool air-conditioning of a downtown cafe.

"Oh, really?" Tabssum shot back on the phone. "Already forgot how dangerous I am? I am capable of sending you down fourteen feet!"

Her words must have broken something inside Bhagyashri because Tabssum heard the girl dissolve into muffled sobs. "Why did Arif do this?" Bhagyashri asked weakly. "I would have never let anything bad happen to him."

After Monika's conversation with Bhagyashri at the train station, she and Arif did not dare turn on their phones again. But her sister's words followed Monika everywhere, wherever this train was taking her, clanking through to its metal spine, rumbling past town after town, filling her with a sinking certainty that her father's heart had really collapsed. Monika believed he would wake only if he saw her at the foot of his hospital bed, but she was going farther and farther away. She wanted to call home, just once, to see if her father answered, but Arif kept warning her that she was getting swept up in Bhagyashri's games again. Monika finally fell asleep, too tired to keep body and heart together.

By the time a stranger named Bajrangi Paji Saheb took interest in their elopement and began tearing through the lives of Arif's relatives and friends, the couple had arrived in Balapur, an ancient village of carpet weavers, to shelter with distant relatives who thought Arif was passing through the region with a classmate on his way to a police training. Within hours, the relatives figured out that Arif and Monika were more than classmates but they did not press them for the real story.

The vast house was on the edge of a lake that shone and sang. But inside, the walls were green with mold. Monika would keep a steel glass aside for herself, irked by everyone's drinking from the same unwashed cup. She would ask for her food to be cooked separately without fats and spices, and wait for someone to mop up the tongue of sewage that crept and pooled at her feet before stepping into the bathroom. At night, she would lay awake for hours, stretched out on a tattered sleeping mat, wedged between an elderly couple and their seven grandchildren, wanting to shake Arif awake to ask what he was dreaming about.

On their first date after marriage, Arif and Monika wandered into a market near the ruins of a medieval fort. The bazaar was a narrow street of small businesses selling diesel in discarded water bottles, a bone-setting service, and handcarts selling earrings and bangles. They stopped at a tailor's shop to buy Monika a burka, and even though the range of styles and silhouettes were unimpressive, she settled on one with heart-shaped velvet embroidery on the back.

Arif watched Monika dreamily as she posed with pouted lips, hands on her hip and hair tossed to the side. He thought she looked more beautiful than ever.

On the way home, Monika tracked Arif's movements from the flapping veil of her new burka, shuffling behind him, sputtering inside this billowing bag of hot air, the bottom of her pregnant stomach suddenly blazing, as he kicked up clouds of dirt, dodged puddles, and skittered over a plank thrown across a river of waste.

"Madam, I know this is very difficult for you," Arif said as Monika lay her head in his lap when they reached home. "I know you are from a very big house, and I know this is not a five-star hotel."

Arif gently tucked the loose strands of her hair behind her ears, cupped her eyes shut, and described a serene beach somewhere far away. Slowly, the dreamy silence carried her to the beach of Arif's imagination, and she felt herself sitting in the sand, resting her head on his shoulder, a soft breeze on their backs, water gurgling at their toes, the sky turning pink. As long as Arif was with her, she would be okay. Suddenly Monika realized she loved him. "I love you," she said and closed her eyes to sleep.

Chapter 10

A Delicate World Toppled

E arly one monsoon morning in September 2017, when Monika
Ingle's eyes opened in the dreamy half darkness of dawn in the
village of Balapur, she swam to her husband, Mohammad Arif Dosani,
on the other end of a sleeping mat. Monika nestled her chin on Arif's
chest and looked for a beautiful sky through the chicken-wire screen of
the kitchen window. She took a moment to notice that dark clouds were
clotting the sky, Arif's body was stiff, his skin was cold, and the delicate
world she had gone to bed in the night before had already toppled over.

"What happened?" She searched Arif's bloodshot eyes. As he
began mumbling his grievances, recounting the news of Monika's family ambushing his family, she felt his words wash over her. Her first
thought was relief—since her father accompanied the Bajrang Dal to
Arif's aunt's house, it meant he was alive; her second thought was irritation that Arif had used a burner SIM card to check on his own family,
even as he had left her to be eaten away by fears about her own. After a

while, as she watched him crumble, his body shaking, his legs flapping, his face vanishing into his palms, she grew ashamed by her inability to say out loud the apologies and reassurances that filled her mind.

"Close your eyes and imagine a wonderful city," she whispered to comfort Arif the way he had consoled her the night before. "We are in a lovely house . . ." Arif looked up at her as if she were possessed and walked away to call his father. She sat up on the sleeping mat, playing with the hem of her kurta, listening to snatches of Arif on the phone outside. Police parties had already fanned out across the state. It was only a matter of time before they kicked open this door and stomped out his dreams.

"Have you ever heard of a police officer charged with a crime?" she heard Arif cry on the phone. "What if they take away my job?"

As the Imamwada Police's forty-eight-hour deadline to bring Arif and Monika home closed in, the shadow of the possibility of a fresh wave of violence grew darker. Arif scanned every face that loomed into view. He kept an anxious eye on neighbors sitting on the balconies of burnt-brick houses, smoking hand-rolled cigarettes at corner shops, milling outside the mosque, to detect the look of casual confidence that no one in this deadbeat village except a plain-clothes police officer was capable of carrying.

When Arif finally sat down to gather himself, it occurred to him that in all the vast sections of the Indian Penal Code he had learned by rote for his police exam, he had never come across a crime known as love marriage. "Sir, you have to do something," Arif begged his lawyer, Vilas Dongre, on the phone. "Otherwise they will destroy us." By evening, Arif had convinced his uncle Rahman to give him a loan so that he could pay Dongre to begin papering the court with petitions to intervene and order an end to the police's harassment of his relatives.

The next morning, Arif's phone beeped with a string of video messages. Dongre stood under a tree outside the court precinct, his black robe folded under an arm, looking anxiously at the crush of news reporters. "The antisocial elements of the Bajrang Dal are disturbing the peaceful lives of my client's family," the attorney read from a sheet of paper. He said that the criminal writ petition he had filed on Arif's behalf argued that since Arif and Monika were both adults, they were not violating any child marriage laws and were, in fact, protected by the fundamental right to freedom of life and liberty guaranteed by article 21 of the Indian constitution. The petition, which named the state of Maharashtra, the police commissioner of Nagpur, the Imamwada Police, and Inspector Amol Jadhav as respondents, asked the court to issue directions to put an end to the couple's harassment and offer police protection from the vigilantes.

When Arif realized that Dongre had snuck in another paragraph, without his permission, seeking compensation of five lakhs of rupees ($7,000) in damages, his heart started pounding. "Instead of protecting ordinary people," Dongre told reporters, "the police accompanied the Bajrang Dal to the house of the boy's relatives at two in the morning, three in the morning, and gave these people a lot of headache."

Even before the news clip was over, Arif had stopped listening. Dongre's words burbled in his ears, and his stomach turned into a clump of knots at the sight of a news crawl throbbing at the bottom of the screen under the lawyer's face: "Nagpur Love Jihad Case . . . Nagpur Love Jihad Case . . . Nagpur Love Jihad Case . . ."

In India, there are two sets of crimes: real and imaginary. Real crimes are the ones that were spelled out in Arif's textbooks, which warranted a clear and defined penalty. Imaginary crimes, on the other hand, were violations of the invisible lines of traditions that were meted out with sentences of shame and guilt that took different forms for a lifetime. Those four reckless words on the news

ticker—"Nagpur Love Jihad Case"—had charged Arif with an attack on Hindu society and pushed him over the edge into the terri-
fying domain of the second category. To make it worse, Dongre was
seeking damages from Monika's family and the Bajrang Dal, giving
them another reason to exact revenge.

"What does this mean?" Monika asked. "'Love Jihad'?"

"That a Muslim boy forced a Hindu girl by making her pregnant,"
he said.

Monika nodded in silence.

"How can these words be used for me?" Arif said in frustration. "I
want to tell everyone that I never forced you to convert to my religion."

"The girl has to convert, baba, she has to," she said. "We asked so
many people. That's what everyone told us."

"We know that, but do they know that?" he said. "Everyone thinks
I am doing love jihad!"

◆────◇────➤

After Arif's petition was filed, Bajrangi Paji Saheb and Inspector Amol
Jadhav went silent. The police vans stationed outside Aunt Akida's
house left Hasanbagh, and Jikar returned home to a spread of mutton
curry and sweet buttered buns. But when Arif sat on a rope cot outside his relatives' house in Balapur, under an open sky, beneath passing
clouds, bathing in the sounds of nature, he could not push the tranquility of his surroundings into his heart. Monika came up with the
plan to change their location every few days: Balapur, Nandura, Selu,
Shegaon—anywhere someone would take them in for a night or two.

Within the next days, Arif's brother-in-law, Zakir, introduced
him to another lawyer, a Muslim who had himself run away with
a Hindu woman. This attorney advised him to withdraw the writ

petition—especially the demand for compensation—in exchange for a written assurance that the police would no longer harass his relatives. "I can see a younger version of myself in you," the man told Arif. "And I call tell you that you will have many problems in life."

Suddenly that afternoon, Monika felt a sharp pain that passed through her body like lightning. Her legs shook, her chest heated up, and she thought her baby would crawl out of her body. Through the hourlong rickshaw ride to a nearby town with an ultrasound machine, Arif held her stomach with both his hands and chanted verses from the Quran. When the doctor injected a syringe into her thigh, Arif also winced.

Since that day she had woken up in this village, and terrible news from Nagpur barged into her dreamy morning, this was the first time Arif had held her hands and looked into her eyes. "Whatever problem comes our way, we will fight it," he told her gently. "Always remember that I am for you, and you are for me."

The following Tuesday, the Imamwada Police filed its reply in court, arguing that since the department was merely performing its duty of investigating a missing person report, Arif's petition was baseless. "It is necessary to produce victim Monika before police station and make the enquiry about said person as maybe abducted under the compulsion to convert her religion against her will and perform the marriage," the document said in the typical garbled English of Indian courthouses. "There is every possibility that the said person might have committed murder of victim Monika as well as there is every possibility that he might have sold her to other person. Therefore investigating officer is making enquiries by all the corners, angles as per reliable sources as well as secret information."

Arif read the document over and over. As he attempted to frame a mind-blowing response using his best English—the lines he would say to the judge, Inspector Jadhav, Bhagyashri, Amit, and Shridhar when they came face-to-face—a new video landed in his in-box. This time Vilas Dongre stood under the gulmohar tree outside the court building distributing a new round of soundbites as though they were wedding sweets.

"I asked the deputy commissioner—'Sir, you have hundreds of missing person complaints on your desk, and you have done nothing about those,'" the attorney said. "'What is so special about this missing person complaint?'"

That afternoon, Dongre put forward Arif's proposal to withdraw the petition in exchange for a written assurance from the police. The court ruled that since the police was compelled to investigate the missing person report and the couple was concerned about their physical safety, Monika would be required to provide her testimony through a video call without having to disclose her location. That same afternoon, Arif's father, Bashir, called with the news that an appointment letter from the Maharashtra Police had arrived in the mail requiring Arif to report to Mumbai within a week for an orientation to secure his constable job.

A second chance at a respectable life, a possibility that had felt so distant in recent days, rested entirely on Monika's testimony on the video call. Detecting doubt and worry on her husband's face, she asked bluntly, "You don't trust me?" Even though Monika promised to tell the truth, Arif could not find it in himself to trust her. He had seen the shock on her face when she understood the kind of poverty he came from. He knew how much she ached to go home. Arif watched Monika's face grow sad as she listened to the lawyer describe how her mother had teared up at his desk. When the day of the video call testimony arrived, Arif made one final plea before leaving the room:

"If you betray me, I will not fight with you, I will not argue, I will not cry. I will leave this world with a smile and tell myself that I lost the biggest gamble of my life by marrying you."

Monika combed her hair, dabbed a fistful of powder on her face, changed into a borrowed top and pair of leggings, and sat down in front of Arif's cell phone. But by the time the public prosecutor on her screen asked her to identify herself, she had turned into a tangle of nerves.

"I am Monika Ingle," she told the court when she finally recalled her name.

"Are you under any compulsion from Mohammad Arif Dosani?" the prosecutor asked.

"No," she answered, patting her face with a pocket handkerchief.

"Are you happy?" the lawyer asked.

"Yes."

"Do you have any problem?"

"Yes," she said firmly. "I have a five-month-old baby in my stomach, and I am facing a lot of difficulty because of the people opposing our marriage. We have to run from this place to that place because I am scared something bad will happen to us."

Monika looked up to see whether her decisive revelation had jolted the prosecutor awake. "Anything else?" he asked.

"No."

The door cracked open, and Arif kissed her all over her face.

◆┄┄◆┄┄◆

A week later, Arif's parents arrived in Balapur to meet their new daughter-in-law. Tabssum took Monika's face in her hands, pressed it against her heaving chest, praised God for blessing her family, and praised herself for raising a son who did not abandon the woman he got pregnant. Monika tried to remember whether she had noticed this peculiar smell—the empty-stomach stench that covered Tabssum's face and hair—the first time she met the woman months earlier when Bhagyashri invited her over for tea and poha. That afternoon, Monika had wandered out into the living room, and Tabssum had noticed her thick hair and wanted to know which hair oil she used. It was only now that she noticed that Tabssum's neck, wrists, and ears were totally bare, without even as much as a thin gold chain.

As Tabssum mumbled into Monika's hair, Arif's father emptied a bag of snacks to mark the happy occasion. There was a savory mix of flattened rice known as *chivda* and a packet of sliced sponge cakes. Bashir had a gray beard that looked like a sprinkling of desiccated coconut and eyes so vacant they reminded Monika of the broken windows of the tumbledown state transport buses that brought them to this village. "Today I want to make a votive," he announced to the family. "If Allah takes the police case away, and our Arif gets his job, I will donate two goats or pay for a poor couple's marriage." Monika glanced around the room to check if anyone else saw the absurdity of her father-in-law's votive; after all, where would Bashir find a couple poorer than him and his wife?

That same afternoon, a favorable court ruling arrived. Arif burst into a dance, chanting the verdict over and over to different tunes, as if it were a new film song. "As the statements of the petitioners are recorded as desired by the respondents, and since the petitioners are not desirous of prosecuting the criminal writ petition in view of the assurance from respondents that they would not take any action against the petitioners," the verdict said, "we dispose of the criminal writ petition with no order as to costs."

Arif was now officially a free man. He imagined himself slicking back his hair, straightening his collar, tossing his sunglasses into the air, and walking out of the shadow of the criminal cases threatening to checkmate his dreams. But Monika was exactly where she had been since she left home. She suddenly felt out of breath, and her smile vanished with the realization that for the next ten days, while her husband attended his police constable orientation in Mumbai, she would have to live with strangers.

As Monika packed their bags, she paused to admire a pair of denim dungarees she had included for a honeymoon that had not yet come. "Ayat, please forgive me, I have to leave you and go toward my future," Arif told Monika, calling her by her new married name. Monika nodded because she did not know how to say that suddenly everyone in this house in Balapur felt unfamiliar, and every moment with them felt like a sting of disappointment in her husband.

"Arif, today our new life has started," Monika wrote in her diary to make a note of all the things she forgot to tell him when they were together. "Do you have proof of my love now or not?" She turned to the biographical page of the diary and thought about who she had become. Name: Ayat Arif Dosani. Residential Address: Arif Papa Home Basmath. Best Subject: English. Best Friend: Arif. Teacher: Arif Dosani. Friend: Arif.

Monika marked every day away from Arif with an entry in the diary. "Arif, today is the third day since you went to Mumbai," she wrote. "I feel as if I have nothing with me except the gift in my stomach that brought us together."

"Arif, today is the fourth day. When you were close to me, I did not say all this, but how would I know that after you leave, every moment would feel like a punishment?"

"Arif, today is the fifth day. I am feeling a lot of weakness, and my health is not good."

"Sixth day. When I take a breath, my wounds feel fresh."

"Today is the festival of Dussehra. I miss my mummy and papa a lot. Everyone at home must be wearing new clothes. Arif, what will Papa be doing? What will Mummy be thinking? Today I am realizing that I am such an unfortunate daughter that I thought about no one but myself and ran away. Everyone must be telling Mummy and Papa something or the other. I wish I was never born, so that my mummy and papa would at least be saved from these taunts. Arif, I don't want to live, I feel like cutting my wrist, please, Arif, please. Arif, for you, I have left everything, my father, mother, brother, sister . . . okay, forget it."

"Arif, I want to go home once. I want to meet everyone. As your begum, as your wife, I want to show them our child. You do one thing: become a police sub-inspector fast-fast, so we can go and meet them, okay? Today it will be one month since I left home, I feel very bad, I feel like crying too much. Sorry, Mummy and Papa."

"Arif, do whatever you want, but please take me from here."

On their tenth morning apart, she ran out of pages.

A month later, Monika traveled to Basmath to live with Arif's family. The rooms were dark and flaking, with nothing except a metal cupboard, a rusted trunk, a sewing machine, and a kitchen shelf. The entrance displayed Tabssum Dosani's hand-stitched creations for sale—sari blouses, brocade borders, petticoats, and swatches of chiffon and silk—hanging on mangled wires that stretched across the frames of two doors. Monika paused to finger the brocade, and her mother-in-law offered to let her drape it on herself.

Monika spent her days listening to Arif's mother read verses from the Quran as she wiped down the kitchen and swept the two-room home. She would sit on the floor, fixed in front of a broken cooler, and fan herself with a *dupatta*, grumbling about power cuts. At the call to prayer, Tabssum would hurtle toward her, clicking her tongue, to cover the young woman's head with a scarf, and Monika would continue chopping vegetables or sorting grains.

A month later, Arif finally returned, bearing a box of sweets. Monika hid her diary because suddenly all her complaints felt irrelevant and inappropriate. Arif showed his wife his new uniform, she tried it on, and they took selfies posing with imaginary revolvers. "Now you won't leave me, right?" she said, pointing her imaginary gun at him. But her smile collapsed the moment she saw the guilty look on his face. Before Arif could start his job in the city, he was required to complete a nine-month training program in Latur, a town deep in the drought belt, a hundred miles away. He would live on the police grounds and get only seven days of leave that year. Since families were not allowed to live on the training grounds, Monika would stay with Arif's family in the village.

Until the ninth month of her pregnancy, Monika found herself in a punishing domestic schedule set by her mother-in-law: cooking, cleaning, filling lunch boxes, emptying them, grinding spices, scrubbing dishes, mopping, dusting, washing and drying clothes. Late at night, she would walk away from her parents-in-law's snoring, rumbling bodies to talk to Arif on the phone or sit in front of a broken fan and think about the Hindi television serials she used to watch at home, predicting their plot twists and turns—even though there was no way to be sure in the absence of a TV. Since Arif left for training, she had stopped writing in her diary because it had become dangerous to put words to the feelings brewing inside her.

One afternoon, a week before she was to give birth, Monika heard

Arif's parents discussing the deposit to admit her to a municipal hospital, and something snapped inside her. She could not sleep, haunted by visions of being left on the stone floor of a crowded corridor of a government hospital, her shrieks drowned out by the cries of other destitutes waiting for medical help. She had heard stories of how doctors in municipal hospitals roughed up pregnant women, pinning them down on rusted tables, slapping their faces to get them to shut up when they yelped in pain, and squeezing babies out of their trembling bodies.

During one of their late-night conversations, Monika told Arif, "It costs five hundred rupees to give birth at the municipal hospital," or $6—the equivalent of a meal at her favorite restaurant in Nagpur. "Or four thousand rupees at a private clinic." Her father spent that amount, equal to $50, on new clothes in the blink of an eye. "What is my life worth to you?"

Arif replied with a cryptic story: "There was this one young woman. She was brilliant, but somehow her dreams never came true. One day, when she was traveling in a train, a gang of armed robbers barged into her compartment, took her luggage, and threw her out of the train," Arif told Monika. "The young woman fell on the tracks, and the train crushed her legs. The whole night, some forty or forty-five trains went over her."

"I am begging you: don't send me to a municipal hospital," Monika replied. "I will find a way to pay you back."

"Let me finish," Arif said. "The woman must have been twenty or twenty-five. Forty or forty-five trains went over her. Just try to imagine that. Imagine what state she must have been in. Her legs had become like minced meat. Some strangers found her squirming on the tracks and took her to the hospital. They were saying, 'Oh, you poor girl, your legs are gone, your dreams are over. Finished.'

139

Doctors, relatives, everyone was saying negative words. All of them were saying negative. negative, negative."

"Please, Arif, I am scared of the municipal hospital," Monika said.

"Let me finish," Arif repeated.

"But why are you telling me this?" she snapped.

"You know what the young woman did?" Arif continued. "She told everyone to leave her alone. For an hour, she thought to herself. She drank a glass of water. A nice cold glass of water. And after one hour, she said, 'I will climb Mount Everest.' You know how tall Everest is? Must be eight or nine kilometers. And you know what? She climbed it. She climbed it even though she did not have legs."

"Okay," Monika said skeptically.

"You know why I told you this story?" Arif finally came to the point. "To make you a little bit more positive. You keep saying, 'Why did I get this? Why not that? Why do I have to get admitted in a municipal hospital? Why not a private clinic?' When you have such thoughts, think of this girl next time. Try to make yourself tough."

Monika hung up the phone and stretched out to sleep. She could not shut out thoughts of what her pregnancy might have looked like if she were at her parents' house. She would have been sleeping in front of a cooler, surrounded by an assortment of stuffed animals, sifting through rompers, toys, and rattles, drinking jugs full of saffron milk sprinkled with cashews and almonds. In the poverty that was her reality, when she had a craving for a lassi from the corner shop, she saw Arif's mother note down the amount, so she could remind her son to return it.

The day Monika went into labor, Arif's parents took her to a private clinic, but Arif was still in training. When she woke up, ripples of pain from seven stitches tore through her body, and she felt her baby scraping at her breast. There was no one by her bedside.

Reshma Mokenwar, a sales assistant from Mumbai, and Preethi
Sarikela, a tailoring student from a village in Telangana, fall
in love and elope together. They move into a slum in Shirdi,
a temple town in western India, pretending to be sisters and
working as hotel staff. When a police team acting on missing
person complaints arrives at their door to take them back to their
families, Reshma and Preethi vow to meet again. "If we can't
live together," Reshma says while handing Preethi shards of a
shattered teacup, "then we'll die together," finishes Preethi.

Chapter 11

A Free Life

Late one afternoon in November 2017, Preethi Sarkila awoke from a short nap. She walked to the bathroom and started to cut her wrist with a sliver of a shattered teacup. She had carried the broken piece with her from Shirdi since the day the men from her village barged into the home she was building with her partner, Reshma Mokenwar. Preethi nudged open the window, watched a line of gray clouds drifting over her hometown of Bazarhathnoor, studied the broken teacup against the weak sun, and thought about how fitting it was that she was ending her life with the relic of an unfulfilled dream.

The last time Preethi saw Reshma Mokenwar, when their families forced them into separate cars after police officers took their signatures and called off the missing persons search, Reshma shouted from the window that they would be together in life or death. As Preethi sawed at her wrist, she recalled those words with a fever-dream slowness, words that now sounded as though they were deliberately full of the unsaid. *They would be together—in this world or another.*

Hours later, as Preethi was being dragged to the doctor to get her wound dressed, she expected Reshma to appear from a bend in the street and grab her. Preethi imagined they would start running madly, feeling the cold winter breeze against their faces, cutting across fields and highways. They would keep on running until wastelands turned into flowering gardens and they reached their room in Shirdi three hundred miles away. They would run inside, fall into bed laughing, and never open the door to another stranger.

When Preethi returned to her parents' house from the doctor, her mother slapped her across the face. Narsa told her that Reshma had gone back to Mumbai. She went on to say that since Reshma had already experienced the pleasures of marriage and sex with men, Reshma had decided to allow Preethi to pursue them herself by promising to not interfere with her arranged marriage. Preethi told her mother to stop talking because she sounded foolish.

Late that evening, Preethi sat with her confusion. It was not like Reshma to succumb to family pressure and sacrifice her love for Preethi. So where the hell was she? Was Reshma scared to call because she worried Narsa and Ushanna would file another police complaint against her? Was she too hurt to come to the village after the terrible accusations of prostitution and kidnapping were hurled at her in front of everybody? Did Reshma hold Preethi responsible for them? Preethi fingered the white gauze on her wounded wrist and wished Reshma knew she had tried to keep her promise to be together in death and how badly she needed to know that Reshma had failed at keeping hers.

On the nineteenth night after Preethi was taken away from her, Reshma lay half asleep, burning with a fever in her parents' home, waiting for morning to come to Friends Colony in Bhandup. When an echo of chants and bells rose inside a nearby temple, Reshma dreamed she was waking up with Preethi to the morning prayer in Shirdi. She sat up, confused and anxious, and looked for the circle of light that fell over her mother's kitchen. She stretched over the sleeping bodies of her brothers and parents, threw on a scarf, and walked out the door.

"*Mumbai Mirror?*" Reshma felt her tongue swell up as she pushed a five-rupee coin across the counter of the corner store.

The *Mirror*, an English-language newspaper she had seen in the hands of important people, such as the madams whose dirty dishes her mother scrubbed and the retired judge her father drove around, contained a photograph of Reshma and Preethi on one of the inside pages. The headline read, "Bhandup Woman Fights Family to Reunite with Her Girlfriend." Reshma's and Preethi's cheeks were pressed together, their bodies in a tight embrace, and their eyes furious and defiant. Even though she had taken this picture herself on the train from Adilabad to Shirdi, with a foldable selfie stick she carried everywhere in her purse, Reshma suddenly felt frightened by it.

A 27-year-old Mumbaikar is up against a rigid set of social and cultural norms that have wrenched her away from her girlfriend.

Reshma Mokenwar, a resident of Bhandup, met her cousin Preethi Sarikela in Telangana last year and fell in love with her. Last year, Mokenwar and Sarikela, 20, eloped to Shirdi in the hope of beginning a new life. The couple worked at a restaurant in Shirdi and stayed in a lodge.

About ten days ago, though, the Telangana Police, acting on a missing person complaint by Sarikela's parents, traced them to Shirdi.

Inspector Jayaram Nayak of the Boath Police Station, in Telangana, said the girls' parents filed missing complaints, since they had left their homes without informing their parents. "Both girls have given us statements that they left their parents' homes since they wanted to work and live on their own."

Days earlier, Reshma had given up eating when news arrived that Preethi's family had arranged her marriage to a cousin from the village. She developed a fever that came and went. Slowly, Reshma's cries turned into whimpers, and she stopped talking altogether.

Her father, Babu, poured two glasses of water and offered Reshma a plastic chair beside his own. He turned to face her, cleared his throat, and asked her what she thought he wanted from life. Was it a house of his own? A beautiful wife? Children who would one day get decent jobs and stop sucking the life out of him? Like every man in the world, all he craved was *izzat*: honor. His face turned soft, and when his frown lines disappeared, her father looked harmless. "It takes a lifetime to earn respect and only a moment to squander it," he said. When Reshma paid attention to her father's sad voice, she thought of a villain from a nineties Hindi movie who woke from a coma and tricked everyone into believing he was changed.

Long after her father stood up and walked away, Reshma thought about him. She had tried before to live a life dictated by his expectations by marrying a man he chose for her, and she had nearly died. For the sake of her father, she had taught herself to float above her body while her husband slept peacefully, an arm thrown over his eyes, moments after she felt that he had forced himself on her.

After a lifetime, Reshma had finally found sleep, long and cool, in Preethi's company. In their weeks together in Shirdi, Reshma often woke suddenly, unable to believe her good fortune. She lifted herself on an elbow simply to watch Preethi dream.

In a voice note to a friend, Reshma rambled, "I struggle for my mummy and papa. Sometimes I think I should listen to them. But how much should I listen to them? Should I obey them even if they are wrong? Why? Sometimes I think I should worry about my own future. In my mind there is a thought: I should live free."

✦┄┄◆┄┄✦

From a window in her parents' home, Reshma watched the sun fill up the sky as millions of copies of the *Mumbai Mirror* swirled throughout the city, carrying millions of testimonies of her love for Preethi. She wondered if someone in the courthouse parking lot had wedged a copy of the paper under the front windshield wipers of her father's car. She imagined the shock on her brother Kishen's face upon finding his colleagues huddled over a photograph of his sister with her life partner. She dreamed that the news had already reached Preethi's village. She fantasized about Preethi's parents calling to say that her groom had changed his mind after reading the newspaper and backed out of the wedding. If Reshma could, she would cover every billboard from Mumbai to Bazarhathnoor with declarations of her love for Preethi.

"All I know is that I don't have any feelings for boys. I have only ever had feelings for girls," Reshma said to her friend. "My heart is always hopeful, it keeps wanting more. After Preethi came into my life, I started thinking, *She is my responsibility, she is my duty, she is mine.*"

The sky turned purple, and the local trains carrying her father and brothers rumbled into the station at the end of the lane. Neither of them had seen the photo of Reshma and Preethi in the paper or read the accompanying article.

Reshma's father changed into his cotton shirt and checked sarong, and sat down for dinner on the plastic chair by the fridge, as her brothers, Kishen and Ganesh, watched music videos on the television. In the rhythms of daily life, Reshma listened for the hum of an impending storm.

The next morning, she woke up to a call from the Tata Institute of Social Sciences, a prestigious graduate school in the city. The voice on the line informed her that Ketaki Ranade, a professor of gender studies and mental health, who worked toward amplifying the voices of lesbian women, had read about her in the *Mirror* and wanted to help her.

Ranade and their team would work with her to get Preethi out of her parents' home as long as she told them herself that she wanted to be with Reshma. A part of Reshma felt confident that now that their love story had pierced the hearts of the English-speaking big people of the city, it would not perish in the anonymity of poverty. It was only a matter of time before Preethi and Reshma found themselves transported back in time to the moment before their world imploded. She imagined Preethi tossing her long, luxuriant hair to one side, pouring two cups of tea in the kitchen of their home in Shirdi. They would take long sips and start their lives again on their terms.

After the call, Reshma was too excited to go back to sleep. Of all the funny English words she had heard before, she had never come across the word the woman caller used: *lesbian*. She looked up the meaning on YouTube and learned that it was a word for a woman who desired another woman. On the phone, the professor's associate said *lesbian* in a whisper, as if trying to gauge whether Reshma was prepared to become visible.

"Lesbian," Reshma said aloud, to hear it in her own voice, as she dressed for a meeting with the professor. She decided that English was a great language because it contained a special word to describe her relationship with Preethi. "Lesbian," she said again and liked the sound of it.

◆━━━◇━━━▶

"I am Preethi," Preethi texted Reshma from a spare cell phone she had stolen from a drawer in her brother-in-law's home. As days slipped away and the date of her arranged marriage to a cousin from the village neared, Reshma's name disappeared from Preethi's home. Whenever she talked about Reshma, a fierce, throbbing silence fell over the house. Her mother would lament an impending drought or the soaring price of cotton seeds, but her tone would turn contemptuous anytime that Reshma's name poisoned the air.

From all the Telugu romantic movies Preethi had watched, she knew that it was painful to lose a beloved to an arranged marriage, but to be the one to be pushed into marriage was to be set on fire. As time passed, the young woman began to experience imaginary physical symptoms of burning. When her mother took her to the tailor to have her wedding sari stitched, her skin broke out in hives. When her father started painting the house before guests arrived, she choked on the fumes of varnish.

"If you are really Preethi, then tell me what you used to call me in Shirdi?" Reshma wrote back. She had also learned from the movies to never trust an unknown number.

"Sonu," Preethi answered.

"What did I call you?" Reshma asked.

"Bacha," Preethi typed.

"What is your other pet name?"

"Sweetie."

"When will you come to get me?" Preethi texted again. "Or we will keep playing *Meelo Evaru Koteeswarudu*"—the Telugu version of *Who Wants to Be a Millionaire*—"till they marry me off?"

Early one winter morning in December 2017, Preethi left for her tailoring class at eight as usual. She took her seat at the sewing machine and waited for her father to wave to her on his way to the fields. At nine forty-five, fifteen minutes before the bus for the nearby town of Ichoda left Bazarhathnoor, she complained of a stomachache and hobbled out of class.

Until eleven, she sat inside a Chinese restaurant in the Ichoda market. Reshma, hidden in a burka, walked into the restaurant, drank a glass of water, and gestured for Preethi to meet her on the mezzanine floor of an office next door, where she too could change into a burka before taking the train to Mumbai.

"Are we really running away wearing burkas?" Preethi dissolved into giggles. "Isn't this a bit too filmy?"

◆┄┄◇┄┄▶

When they arrived in Mumbai, Reshma and Preethi took a rickshaw to a shelter for homeless women in a crumbling part of the city, where friends of Professor Ranade had made arrangements for them to stay. Women who looked like ghosts of a happier time were heaped in boiling rooms with walls painted in cheerful, bright colors as an exercise in therapy to process the grief of domestic abuse, trafficking, murder attempts, harassment, and abandonment. All day long, the women sat scattered across the shelter in silence, caught in the grim repetitions of daily life, studying their parted hair for lice, hanging clothes from dark window grilles, staring into the middle distance, and listening to motivational songs that played in a loop. It was the kind of gloom that seeped into the skin and continued to linger underneath for a long time afterward.

Reshma and Preethi leapt at the first opportunity to interview for jobs at a data entry business as part of the not-for-profit's efforts to provide livelihoods to destitute women. The office of the data entry business was closed for renovation, but the owner offered them a stipend to supervise construction workers for a month until the remodeling was done.

The two lovers escaped the gloom of the shelter to hold hands on the steps outside the data entry office. As jackhammers, motors, chop saws, welding machines, and electric saws thundered inside, they would rest their heads on each other's shoulders and scroll through A Free Life, a WhatsApp group of queer couples that Professor Ranade's associates had invited them to join. A young woman police officer from rural Maharashtra talked about struggling with the desire to be open about her sexual identity for fear of losing her job. Two professors told the group about workshops they conducted on queer affirmative mental health. An elderly community teacher from the countryside wanted to know if anyone could introduce her to a woman who was interested in becoming her life partner. The group discussed the cultural silence around homosexual desire, the myth that lesbians were only urban and educated women, and the tragedy of women's sexual experiences always being discussed only in the context of reproduction and childbearing. The women talked about how Section 377, the colonial-era law that criminalized homosexual desire, did not specifically include lesbianism because its focus was on outlawing penetrative sex, and that itself was another way to invalidate the existence of women who desired women. The members spoke excitedly about finally freeing themselves from living with half-truths and promised to support one another in accepting the full facets of their sexual identity.

Reshma spoke up. "I don't know anything about the law or the constitution," she said. "I have only one dream in my life: that I should have a house somewhere where Preethi and I can be happy. It should have a small shrine of Sai Baba, and I should have so much money that I can give her everything she wants." Reshma had noticed that many of the lesbian couples who lived together settled happily into roles as husband and wife, with one partner assuming a more masculine identity and the other taking on feminine duties. "Preethi should never have to feel she needs to look outside our marriage. Then we will be *taka-tak*, tip-top, no problem," Reshma finished.

When their contract with the data entry business expired, Reshma and Preethi decided to move back to Shirdi to restart their lives together. On Mahashivratri in February 2018, Reshma called her mother to say that she and Preethi were coming over to the Friends Colony to say good-bye before they left.

That afternoon, as Reshma parted the cloth curtain of the entryway to her family's home, the house shook with seismic laughter. Reshma's brothers, Kishen and Ganesh, collapsed on the floor, clutching their stomachs, the pitch of their laughter rising in competition.

"What have you done to yourself?" Reshma's mother, Rekha, turned to her, suppressing the laughter bubbling inside her.

"What?" she answered. Reshma had given herself a crew cut and stained the tips of her hair with henna. She wore long Bermuda shorts, the kind her brothers wore out to the lane when they played cricket or smoked at the corner store. She had thrown out her slippers for big rubber sandals, put away her earrings and gold chains, and switched to a men's wallet that she slipped into her back pocket.

"You know what the word *chakka* means?" Reshma's brother Kishen stumbled across the room, laughing like a happy drunk. "Your transformation to a bloody eunuch is complete."

"Shut your filthy mouth." Reshma pushed her brother aside.

"You gave up everything to become a *chakka*!" Kishen roared, burying his head in their mother's shoulder to continue laughing.

Chapter 12

Take Me as I Am

O ne summer evening in May 2018, three months after Reshma Mokenwar and her girlfriend Preethi Sarikela moved to Shirdi for a second time, Reshma asked Preethi if Reshma was enough for her. Preethi, in a cotton top and harem pants, was bent over to open the brass padlock of their room in one of the lanes behind the Sai Baba Temple, as usual after the last prayer at nine thirty. Lately, since they started spending time apart working in separate hotels, Reshma could never be sure if Preethi's silence was deliberate or accidental. There was no way to tell if her voice suddenly stopped reaching Preethi or if she had decided that she answered enough questions. Usually Reshma filled the stillness with more questions, but the thought of Preethi choosing to be mute in the face of her vulnerability stunned her into silence.

Preethi left her rubber slippers at the door, hung her purse on the wall, tucked the loose strands of her hair back into her plait, and walked over to the kitchen to warm the rice and curry she had cooked before leaving for work. Preethi tried to do most of her cooking in the hour before sunrise so that she could come home from the hotel and watch her Telugu serials in peace. Reshma thought about asking the question again, which had lingered all day like the half memory of a late-morning dream—*Was she enough?*—but she decided that it was foolish. If she could learn to love Preethi cleverly, she would have to be enough.

"Your boss told me she hears you laughing a lot these days," Reshma said as she drew circles in her rice and curry.

"I try to be happy." Preethi looked up from her plate. "That way days don't seem so long."

"You are happy because I am not with you or because your boyfriend is with you?" Reshma knew this was not a clever way to love, but the thought of Rahul, a server who flirted with all the women at the budget lodge where Preethi worked in housekeeping, made her feel like she was going insane. One day when Reshma noticed the way Rahul devoured Preethi with his hungry eyes, she took him aside to tell him that Preethi was her girlfriend. He laughed and squirmed like she had tickled the back of his neck with a feather. When Reshma's face grew severe and unforgiving, he hiked up his jeans and walked away.

It frustrated Reshma that ever since she had left the budget hotel to take a job in room service at City Heart, a three-star hotel where tips were bound to be generous because it was preferred by the more fortunate of Sai Baba's devotees, it had become harder to protect Preethi from the men orbiting around her. She wanted so badly for Preethi to understand that if she laughed too easily, if she forgave unwanted attention, they would come back for more.

"I am trying to be happy even though you are not with me," Preethi answered. She got up to wash her plate but scraped it and left it in the sink to soak till the morning. She unfurled her sleeping mat and stretched out with her phone to start the serials. Reshma thought about asking Preethi why she did not like talking anymore, but Preethi refused to look up and give her the chance to start another fight.

◆┈┈◇┈┈➤

In the hours before dawn, Reshma woke suddenly and struggled to fall asleep again. "I'm trying to be happy even though you are not with me," Preethi had said to her the night before. There was something slippery inside her words, as if she said something but meant something else, that made Reshma feel cheated.

A thousand times, Reshma told Preethi to call when she got a break at work. A thousand times she told her to wear a scarf and tie her hair into a modest plait because men interpreted the absence of these things as sexual provocations. A thousand times, she told her that she did not like it when Preethi laughed too easily with strangers. A thousand things a thousand times, but they were not enough.

Were there any couples who were enough for each other? When she thought about her own family, she thought of Ganesh, the brother who married a woman of their mother's choice but may have continued to look for comfort in the dim red rooms of sex workers. Kishen, the brother who kept his girlfriend of a half decade waiting for marriage, hoping for his luck to change. It was amazing to Reshma that despite all her father's cruelties, he had always been enough for her mother. She had stood in awe of him because she had been frightened by him. In all the years of their marriage, Rekha had never laughed too easily with strangers.

The whole morning, Reshma thought about her father. As she flattened her chest into a tight sports bra to get dressed for work, she realized that her father was enough for her mother because he was enough for himself. As she stepped into a pair of knee-length shorts, she decided that she would learn to believe it herself. She bowed to a poster of Sai Baba and drew a crescent moon with sandalwood paste on her forehead, where the third eye was said to reside.

In July 2018, six months after Reshma and Preethi eloped a second time to restart their lives together, five judges of the Supreme Court convened in New Delhi to hear a slew of public interest litigations that revived a three-decade-old debate on the constitutional validity of Section 377, the colonial-era law that criminalized sexual acts "against the order of nature" and lumped homosexuality with bestiality and pedophilia.

The petitioners included a classical dancer from Punjab, a motivational speaker from Karnataka, a celebrity chef from New Delhi, an activist from Lucknow, a journalist from Mumbai, and a collective of students and graduates from the prestigious Indian Institutes of Technology.

Over four days, the judges heard arguments about whether Section 377 infringed on the fundamental rights to life and liberty. They deliberated whether the law was an affront to the dignity of the country's lesbian, gay, bisexual, and transgender population, even if there was no evidence of prosecutions in police and judicial records.

Did a law that equated homosexuality with bestiality and pedophilia have a place in the twenty-first century? If Lord Macaulay, the British historian who drafted the law in 1838, recognized a lesser sentence for homosexual acts performed with consent, why was there was no consideration of consent within the framework of the law two centuries later? If the right to privacy was a fundamental right, wasn't sexual orientation an essential component of identity? Could the questions of gender identity and sexual orientation be untangled? Was the fear of persecution under this law being used to silence lesbian, gay, bisexual, and transgender victims of discrimination, violence, or sexual assault?

The judges discussed how other countries, especially the United Kingdom, South Africa, the United States, Canada, and Nepal, safeguarded the rights of their lesbian, gay, bisexual, and transgender populations. In Canada, the Supreme Court noted that homosexuality was "a deeply personal characteristic that was either unchangeable or changeable only at unacceptable personal costs." They considered the words of the US Supreme Court justice Anthony Kennedy, who noted that "the generations that wrote and ratified the Bill of Rights and Fourteenth Amendment did not presume to know the extent of freedom in all its dimensions, and so they entrusted to future generations a charter protecting the right of all persons to enjoy liberty as we learn its meaning."

They heard members of various religious organizations who argued that homosexuality was "against the order of nature" and asked them their interpretations of its meaning. They heard members from the Indian Psychiatric Society who said that homosexuality was not a mental disorder. They debated whether striking down the law would destabilize the institution of heterosexual marriage. Would it lead to a surge in sexually transmitted diseases? Would it encourage incest? Would people suddenly say they were attracted to their sisters and brothers? Was there still some wisdom in preserving a relic of Victorian morality in modern-day India? What did ancient Indian scriptures say about homosexual behavior?

In the end, there was one question that loomed above all the other debates: Should majoritarian morality matter more than constitutional morality?

◆————◇————▶

Three months later, in September 2018, Chief Justice Dipak Misra delivered the court's historic ruling that homosexuality would no longer be a crime. "Not for nothing," he began, "the great German thinker Johann Wolfgang von Goethe had said, 'I am what I am, so take me as I am.'"

A phalanx of reporters and photographers camped out on the Supreme Court lawns, muttering into their earpieces, thumbs skittering over their phones, and adjusting their lenses, as they waited to hear updates as the biggest news story of their careers was unfolding inside.

At midday, Justice Misra read down one of the world's oldest bans on homosexuality, announcing that criminalizing gay sex was irrational, indefensible, and arbitrary. With the verdict, every gay, lesbian, bisexual, and transgender citizen would have the same constitutionally guaranteed rights and protections as any other Indian, he said.

"The society has changed much now, not just from the year 1860, when the Indian Penal Code was brought into force, but there has also been continuous progressive change," said Misra. "In many spheres, the sexual minorities have been accepted. But the offense punishable under Section 377 IPC, as submitted, creates a chilling effect. The freedom that is required to be attached to sexuality still remains in the pavilion, with no nerves to move. The immobility due to fear corrodes the desire to express one's own sexual orientation as a consequence of which the body with flesh and bones feels itself caged and a sense of fear gradually converts itself into a skeleton sans spirit.

"The sexual autonomy of an individual to choose his or her sexual partner is an important pillar and an insegregable facet of individual liberty. When the liberty of even a single person of the society is smothered under some vague and archival stipulation that it is against the order of nature or under the perception that the majority population is peeved when such an individual exercises his or her liberty despite the fact that the exercise of such liberty is within the confines of his or her private space, then the signature of life melts, and living becomes a bare subsistence, and, resultantly, the fundamental right of liberty of such an individual is abridged," Justice Misra wrote.

"Section 377 IPC does not meet the criteria of proportionality and is violative of the fundamental right of freedom of expression, including the right to choose a sexual partner. Section 377 IPC also assumes the characteristic of unreasonableness, for it becomes a weapon in the hands of the majority to seclude, exploit, and harass the LGBT community. It shrouds the lives of the LGBT community in criminality, and constant fear mars their joy of life. They constantly face social prejudice, disdain, and are subjected to the shame of being their very natural selves. Thus, an archaic law which is incompatible with constitutional values cannot be allowed to be preserved."

As the chief justice read the judgment inside a room in the Supreme Court, a cheer went up on the lawns, and the tide of photographers surged toward a young woman who unfurled a rainbow flag. The next day's newspaper headlines screamed, "India Makes History!" "Pride, Not Prejudice!" "Momentous Verdict!" "Bid Adieu to Prejudices!"

In Bangalore, people danced and kissed on the steps of a courthouse. In Chennai, chocolates were distributed at traffic lights. In New Delhi, hotel staff broke into a flash mob to celebrate the verdict. In Mumbai, in a shower of confetti, people marched with "I Am Gay" painted on their cheeks. In Gujarat, a gay prince declared that India had finally won independence. In Shirdi, however, the news did not interrupt the rhythms of Reshma and Preethi's daily life.

◂┄┄◆┄┄▸

The week of the verdict, when Reshma arrived at the budget hotel with two cups of tea and a plate of spiced guava to surprise Preethi, she was not in the kitchen. The staff bathrooms were empty. She was not behind the water tank on the mezzanine floor where she liked to sit and edit her selfies into romantic music videos. The cook said there had been no new order to be delivered to the guest rooms.

"Must be with Rahul," he added.

Reshma put down the cups and let the guavas soak the newspaper they were wrapped in. "Why would she be with Rahul?"

"Full day some drama is going on between them," he replied.

"What do you mean?"

"She gave him a love letter," he said. "After that, she started crying . . ."

Just then, Rahul and Preethi appeared at the kitchen door. Rahul
was talking into his phone, wearing a printed shirt over jeans that
hung low to reveal the red band of his briefs. Preethi carried a tray
of dirty plates to the sink, smiling at Reshma and the spiced guavas.

Reshma wanted to grab Rahul by the collar, throw him in the
dirt, and beat him. She knew men like him, she had grown up
among them, she had married and divorced them. She knew how
they took advantage of women. When their advances were rejected,
they found ways to torment them. She wanted to tear his eyes out.
She wanted to take the phone that was stuck to his ear and shove
it down his throat. She wanted to pick up a rubber hose and thrash
him.

"What is this that I just heard?" she asked Rahul. When she heard
her voice, she was ashamed at how unmenacing it sounded outside
her head. "Why are you spreading lies that Preethi gave you a love
letter?"

"Want to see?" He held out a folded notebook paper covered in
Preethi's handwriting. His voice was cheerful, and his teeth were
shining.

By the time Preethi finished washing the cutlery and patted her
hands dry, the tea had turned cold, and the guavas had gone black.
Reshma had already slipped into the evening prayer crowd and disappeared without saying good-bye.

◄┄┄┄◆┄┄┄►

In the evening, Preethi came home from work after the last prayer and hung her purse on the wall. She left her slippers at the door and walked to the stove to warm rice and curry for dinner. Her luxurious, long hair swung at her hips as she moved around the kitchen. She set out two plates on the floor and explained that the letter had been a misunderstanding.

In the restlessness of boredom that morning, Preethi had torn a paper from the hotel notepad and started to write a love letter to Reshma. When the phone rang, she flipped the paper over and took down a guest's order for room service. She said that she realized her mistake only after she had already passed the slip over to Rahul to process the order.

Reshma's head grew heavy, her chest felt tight, and her eyes began to sting. She could not speak even though Preethi was prepared to answer every one of her questions this time.

"Why did you leave without meeting me?" Preethi whispered to Reshma.

Reshma stirred her irritation into her rice and curry as Preethi's banal laments acquired a flammable quality. Preethi said that Rahul had made the letter a big deal, passing it around in the kitchen, when he knew it was not intended for him. She said she had burned with embarrassment and begged him to stop, but he refused to listen. Reshma suddenly looked up from her plate and examined a hair that had fallen in her food. This time when Reshma saw Preethi, she saw a beautiful face framed by loose bangs she had cut herself. *How arrogant Preethi is about her beauty*, she thought.

In their early days together, when they had nothing, and their stomachs rumbled with hunger, Preethi had insisted on buying a bottle of hair oil instead of a packet of biscuits. *What would she be without her hair? Who would love her? Would she be enough?* Preethi would know how lucky she was to have Reshma only if she was stripped of her arrogance. Reshma walked to the kitchen, grabbed a knife, and lopped off Preethi's plait.

PART THREE

Dawinder Singh and Neetu Rani, young lovers from a village in the northern Indian state of Haryana, take shelter with the Love Commandos, a group of vigilantes that protects couples marked for honor killings by their families. As days pass, it becomes clear they have landed in the grip of morally ambiguous journalist-activists seeking to profit off their vulnerability. As Neetu and Dawinder debate leaving the shelter, the murders of Manoj and Babli Banwala, lovers from a nearby village whose bodies are found in tattered gunnysacks, serve as a grim reminder of what can happen to young people who defy caste tradition.

Chapter 13

Within Yourself Make Patience the Bow

E arly one morning in January 2017, the day after they left the Love Commandos shelter, Neetu Rani and Dawinder Singh wandered through the lane behind the Tis Hazari Courts in Old Delhi to inspect lawyers for hire who had set up shop on the footpath outside the court complex. The attorneys, who called themselves advocates, solicitors, and legal consultants, chained their chairs to their desks to keep them from being stolen. They stuck their business cards behind the wipers of parked cars and carried ink pads in the pockets of their dress pants.

When a flock of flapping black coats gathered around Neetu and Dawinder, sensing an opportunity for business, Dawinder showed a photograph of the temple wedding the Love Commandos had organized three months earlier. But before he could even finish explaining that they needed legal help for the final step of registering their marriage, the crowd had scattered. The temple wedding was the most lucrative part of the process, and the task of registration for a ceremony that took place three months earlier was too much work for too little money.

"It'll be ten thousand rupees for the whole headache again," one of the black coats said as he returned to his perch on a stool. Anyone in their right mind would get the user name and password from whoever facilitated the temple wedding—bribing them if they needed to be persuaded—and register the marriage once and for all instead of taking on the hassle of repeating the process. "What's the deal, brother?" the attorney asked when he saw Dawinder's face shrink with worry.

Although Dawinder had expected the question, it was still uncomfortable to attempt an explanation. There was no short answer for why it was easier to wipe out the last of his father's savings and get married again for less than a fifth of the amount he had already paid the Love Commandos than take on the task of convincing Sanjoy Sachdev to part with the information.

"It's a long story," he answered.

Three days later, Neetu and Dawinder waited for his parents, Gurmej Singh and Sukhwinder Kaur, to arrive at a temple in Ghaziabad, a town on the outskirts of New Delhi. When Dawinder saw his father turn a corner from the bus stand, wearing a baggy sweater, old-fashioned square glasses wedged into his wrinkled face, a folded plastic bag containing the last of his savings pressed under his arm, he thought he might start to cry. His mother hobbled behind his father, looking even smaller than he remembered, wearing the same old tattered slippers and blue kurta and pajama pants that had faded to a dirty white in the wash.

Later that afternoon, Neetu and Dawinder exchanged garlands, circled a holy fire seven times, and vowed to be together for seven births for a second time that winter. By evening, the wedding was registered and the couple was, at last, legally husband and wife. When Neetu veiled her head with the loose end of her *dupatta* and touched her new parents-in-law's feet to seek their blessings, Sukhwinder Kaur pulled her up by the shoulders and wished her a long and happy married life.

After the wedding, the family went to a Sikh temple to rest until the morning. Late that night, Neetu woke up to find her mother-in-law pressing her feet. "What did I do to deserve your love?" Neetu said as she covered her face with her hands and started to cry. Dawinder sat up beside her and patted her back to console her.

The next day, the newlyweds left for his aunt Kulwant Kaur's home in a nearby state because it was clear that only harm awaited them in Kakheri. Gurmej Singh and Sukhwinder Kaur returned to their village with the intention of selling their house. Someday, they told one another, they would all go far away and live together in peace.

◄—◄——◊——►—►

In March Neetu and Dawinder were sitting down for dinner when the phone rang. Dawinder's parents had returned home from visiting a relative and found their home in ruins. The backdoor had been busted open, trunks full of clothes and valuables were empty, the TV was shattered, kitchen shelves were ransacked, and the jambool tree in the courtyard was slashed. Electrical switchboards were cracked open, live wires were left dangling, the water tank had disappeared, and photos of the family lay torn into pieces on the floor.

That afternoon, as Gurmej Singh waited to meet the officer in charge at the Siwan Police Station to report the damage, Sukhwinder Kaur overheard Neetu's mother, Sudesh Rani, talking on the phone near the courtyard, asking for jeeps full of relatives to come with whatever weapons they could get their hands on.

An hour later, when Dawinder's mother heard a commotion, she locked herself inside her son's room. As the voices grew louder, she threw her weight against the door and covered her mouth to stifle her cries, but the door flung open, and Neetu's father, Kala, dragged her out to the lane by the hair. Kala clutched an axe; his brothers wielded knives and bamboo sticks. Sudesh Rani was carrying a sickle, and Ruksana, Neetu's younger sister, came with an iron rod.

The women shoved her roughly to the ground, held her down, and twisted her arms. Then the men began flogging her, continuing even as her screams grew faint, and she drifted in and out of consciousness. All the while, a group of neighbors stood watching like mourners at a funeral site. Eventually she vomited and passed out with her face in the dirt, and someone in the crowd suggested that she might be dead. After Neetu's family stalked off, the neighbors carried Sukhwinder Kaur to her courtyard.

Two hours later, when Gurmej Singh returned to Kakheri, his wife was inconsolable. Her face was covered in gashes. Her legs were swollen like columns, her fingers were smashed, her neck was frozen, and her arm was twisted out of its socket.

"I asked them for water. I was crying and crying," she sobbed. "You know what they told me? That they will piss in my mouth."

Gurmej Singh sat on the edge of the bed and watched his wife cry. After a while, he removed his glasses and wiped them with his shirt. "Within yourself make patience the bow," he said finally, quoting a verse from the Guru Granth Sahib, the holiest scripture in Sikhism. "And make patience the bowstring."

That night, doctors in a government clinic in a nearby town counted a total of eleven severe blunt-force traumas to Sukhwinder Kaur's legs, arms, hips, and head, and admitted her for treatment. Her husband sat by her hospital bed and read passages from the Guru Granth Sahib until she drifted to sleep. After nine, he left her sleeping and rode his motorcycle back to the police station to register a complaint against Neetu's father, Gulzar Singh; her uncles Darbara Singh and Shisha Singh; her mother, Sudesh Rani; and her sister, Ruksana.

◆┄┄◇┄┄▸

Three weeks later, the day Sukhwinder Kaur was discharged from the hospital, Gurmej Singh heard from neighbors that no arrests had been made. Kala and his brothers were at their firewood shop eating lunch from shining steel tiffin boxes. Sudesh Rani was hosing down her buffaloes and leading a prayer group. Ruksana was stretched out in front of the television.

Three years before, when Gurmej Singh gave up his driving job because of the strain on his eyes, he had dreamed of growing old in his father's paddy fields. After the attack, he became sure that it was best to sell their ancestral land and move to another village. But with Kala and his family still roaming free, it was impossible to find a buyer for a property that had become the site of a community feud.

"The local police has not taken any action against the accused persons for the last more than twenty-five days, and the accused persons are wandering freely in the village." Gurmej Singh paid a stenographer to type up letters of grievance to police officials and the chief minister in the futile hope that someone would read them.

As days passed without a word from officials and his savings starting to dry up, Gurmej Singh decided that eating one meal per day was sufficient. Days turned into weeks, and relatives whose houses Gurmej Singh and Sukhwinder Kaur had been shuttling between for a half year started to ask about their long-term plans.

Every few days, he rode his motorcycle six hours to the Punjab and Haryana High Court in the city of Chandigarh to explore legal options. "How much will it cost to apply for police protection?" he asked a lawyer who was distributing business cards on the lawns outside court one afternoon. "We want to go to our house and sell it once and for all."

The lawyer ran up to his desk at the end of a dark corridor, made notes of the case file, photocopied the police report, took an advance of the payment to file a petition for police protection, and promised to be in touch. After a week, he stopped answering the phone.

◆┄┄◇┄┄➤

Late one morning in April 2017, Neetu sat on a bed in her aunt-in-law Kulwant Kaur's sprawling bungalow in the countryside, in a matching pajama suit, looking like she had seen a ghost. She had woken from a nightmare in which she saw herself at Dawinder's feet. She kept telling him she would die without him, but he kicked her and walked away to be with his parents.

Since the day she received word of her family beating her mother-in-law, Neetu was tormented by nightmares every time she closed her eyes to sleep. When she forced herself to stay awake, she felt so physically sick from worrying, she started to vomit. For days after the news came, she had been unable to keep down food. After a while, she did not have the energy to walk to the bathroom to vomit, so she kept a plastic bucket next to her bed.

The day Dawinder insisted on taking her to a doctor, she discovered she was pregnant. Neetu thought her husband would burst with happiness, but as soon as they reached home, the celebrations were eclipsed by worries about her mother-in-law's hospital bills and their unsold ancestral property. Although a buyer had been found for their rice and wheat fields—at half the market price—no one was willing to consider buying the house, fearing its proximity to Kala. The longer Neetu's family stayed out of prison, the harder it would be for Dawinder's parents to sell the property and leave the village.

Dawinder called Sanjoy Sachdev, the chairman of the Love Commandos, in a final bid of desperation that afternoon.

"Good afternoon, Baba." He winced as he spoke because he knew that before long, the conversation would become unpleasant.

"Dawinder?" Sachdev answered good-naturedly, as if they had parted on friendly terms. "Long time. How are you?"

Dawinder took advantage of the man's good mood and explained that Neetu's family had broken into his parents' house and attacked his mother, but the police refused to make arrests in the case. He said he knew the Love Commandos had connections in the police force across northern India, and if there was anyone who could save them, it was only the Commandos.

"I told you not to leave the shelter, but you people didn't listen," Sachdev said.

Dawinder waited in guilty silence.

"Send me the FIR copies," Sachdev said. The first information report, a document filled out by the police when they receive information about a cognizable offense, was the foundation for setting the criminal justice process in motion. Then he added, "Tell me— you have any money?"

When Dawinder explained that their savings had been depleted, and they were living with relatives, Sachdev complained suddenly of poor cell phone reception and said he would call back later.

"Today our whole day went in thinking about what should be done about the situation at home," Neetu wrote in her diary later that night. "Dav was happy that he is going to become a papa, but he could not show it."

◆┄┄◇┄┄►

For most of April, a heat wave gripped northern India. Water disappeared from the earth, and the offices of public officials were crowded with farmers from the scorched countryside seeking irrigation supply.

A clerk in the Office of the Director General of Police perked up while reading Gurmej Singh's petition, which must have stood out among the drudgery of files about water shortages. "Why did she run away?" he asked. "These girls don't think twice before destroying families."

Gurmej Singh nodded and inquired when the police chief would begin accepting visitors. He fully expected to leave with nothing. If he had learned anything from weeks waiting in the corridors of government offices, it was that justice was an illusion for a poor man in India, especially if your son took a girl from the same village.

After a three-hour wait, Police Chief Muhammad Akil invited Gurmej Singh into his air-conditioned cabin. A broad-shouldered man with hard, black eyes and a pencil mustache, Akil was the first official who listened carefully, asked questions about the police complaint, and jotted down details in his notepad.

"You are our last hope," Gurmej Singh said despairingly. His hands trembled, and tears streamed down his face. Even though he had pleaded with numerous government and police officials in the months since Neetu and Dawinder eloped, a tide of emotion swept over him each time he narrated the events that led to the assault on his wife. He told Chief Akil that he believed local officials had accepted a bribe from Neetu's family to hush up the complaint. "They left my wife to die," he said in a quavering voice.

Akil pushed a box of tissues across the table. Gurmej Singh rose from his chair and waited to be dismissed. "The arrests will be made," Akil said matter-of-factly. "A team of police officers will escort you back to your house tomorrow."

On the morning of April 25, hours after Neetu's father and uncles were arrested, the flour mill shops at the Kakheri bazaar came grinding to a halt when Dawinder's parents rode into the village on the back of police motorcycles. At the time, Neetu's mother was walking her buffaloes out of the shed, and her sister was piling rolled-up mattresses and bulging sacks of utensils and clothes. Until Kala was released from jail, Sudesh Rani and Ruksana had decided to live out in a shack on their fields for safety.

"How long will you hide behind these policemen?" Sudesh Rani fixed Sukhwinder Kaur with a stare as she walked out. A tide of neighbors gathered to watch the confrontation. Some of them climbed onto their rooftops to watch the fight. "It is a matter of time before my husband kills all four of you. Even if you are hiding in hell," Sudesh Rani went on.

Gurmej Singh thought his neighbors might have been jerked back to their senses. He assumed they had gathered to broker a truce between the two families now that it was clear that even if their son's elopement felt like a crime, the law was really on his side. But then he heard someone in the crowd suggest that Gurmej Singh and his wife should be thrown out of the village.

The neighbors said it was a pity that the Sikhs had first taken a girl from the village and now had a respectable family thrown in jail. If boys and girls from the same village kept running away without consequence, the foundation of society would crumble. Gurmej Singh and Sukhwinder Kaur, sensing more trouble, hurried into their house, followed silently by the two constables Chief Akil had assigned to protect them.

Later that day, Gurmej Singh went back to Siwan Police Station to ask why Sudesh Rani and Ruksana, whose names were in the first information report for attacking his wife, had not been arrested.

Jitender Kumar, the inspector in charge, was surrounded by a group of wealthy upper-caste men from neighboring villages who were seeking his advice on a property matter. Kumar, as usual, was stretched out on a stack of mattresses in his undershirt, poking around the inside of his ear with his little finger. His khaki uniform hung on a hook over his desk.

"The big man is here," Kumar announced when he saw Gurmej Singh and gestured at him to sit down.

"Sir, what about the women?" Gurmej Singh said. "Kala's wife and daughter."

"Let's see," the inspector said.

Gurmej Singh explained that he believed that Neetu's family had acquired illegal weapons that could be used to harm them. He worried that Neetu's brother, a marine commando in the Indian Navy, would return to the village to take revenge.

"Already we have given you two men for free," Kumar said, annoyed. "Is that not enough?"

As Gurmej rose to leave, Kumar smiled and ordered a round of tea. "Before you go," he said, "tell me one thing: How did your stars become so bright that they shone right above the big offices of Chandigarh?"

"When God wants something to happen," Gurmej said, folding his hands, "He finds a way."

◆·····◆·····➤

A week later, the constables assigned to protect Dawinder's parents stopped coming to work. The governor was visiting a nearby town, and they were required to join his security cover. In any case, inspector Jitender Kumar decided that Gurmej Singh and Sukhwinder Kaur had been given protection long enough to gather their things and leave. They were no longer in danger, he determined, even though Kala and his brothers were already out on bail.

One evening, when Gurmej Singh walked home from the market, he was overcome with a strange and nameless fear. The sky had turned a deep purple, and shutters were clanking down for the day. At the corner, Kala was sitting in a tea shop, taking long sips of milky tea. Their eyes met, held each other for a moment, and Gurmej Singh felt a flare of fear leap up to his throat. When he reached home that night, he sat down on the floor and wept.

Days later, in June 2017, when the buyer who had shown interest in the house backed out, Gurmej Singh and Sukhwinder Kaur packed their belongings in backpacks, gunnysacks, and shopping bags. They locked the gate to their house and took a bus out of the village.

Chapter 14

Love Marriage = Destroy Life

L ate one morning in April 2017, Kulwant Kaur, the youngest of Dawinder Singh's aunts, gathered the family in the living room of her sprawling bungalow to discuss the attack on her sister. She was a veterinarian's wife with jet-black hair and loose, wrinkled skin who prided herself on taming feral daughters-in-law within the first weeks of marriage. The matches for both her sons, Bunty Singh and Shanty Singh, were handpicked from resumes of eligible young women that crowded her kitchen platform for months before she decided it was time for them to settle down. One of the weddings had taken place over video call while her son was still working abroad, but the matches had proved so successful that they resulted quickly in a stream of grandchildren.

Neetu Rani and Dawinder Singh sat in guilty silence in plastic folding chairs as Aunt Kulwant Kaur hunched over the center teapoy to fill up their cups. The room had a maroon carpet, life-size

179

posters of her sons posing under the London Bridge, and wall decor featuring miniature Victorian columns. As she was offering biscuits on a tray to Dawinder and Neetu, she said, "I tell everybody: 'Look at this marriage and straighten up. Otherwise, you should go and jump in a well. Before you kill your parents this way, you should go and die.'"

"*Baap re baap.*" Her husband clucked his tongue sympathetically and took a long sip of tea. "No one should do something like this."

"I'm telling you it was this girl Neetu who made our Dawinder do all this," Kulwant Kaur went on, implementing one of her signature strategies for reining in a new daughter-in-law by talking about her as if she were not in the room. "Our boy is so timid, it makes you wonder whether he even has a tongue inside his mouth. No chance he would have run if she did not force him."

Dawinder stared out of the window and nodded. He worried that if he interrupted his aunt to defend himself or his wife, she would become so swept up in her anger that she would forget the crucial task of instructing his middle aunt to leave for Kakheri to settle his mother's hospital bills.

"All their property was worth lakhs of rupees," Kulwant Kaur said. "It will have to be sold at dirt because of this Dawinder's stupid mistake."

Kulwant Kaur's family lived in a place known as NRI village, for the number of nonresident Indians it exported to the United States, United Kingdom, Europe, and Australia. The village was dotted with sprawling holiday mansions overlooking mustard farms that were built by former residents who earned in dollars and pounds. Young boys from the village who were unable to get a visa to move abroad, such as Kulwant Kaur's younger son, Shanty, were known pitifully as *kacha*: unripe. Years after he stopped trying to get a visa, Shanty remained so tormented about being *kacha* that his eyes would well up whenever he heard about another young man leaving to go abroad. Dawinder was the rare species who had thrown away the opportunity to settle in the United Kingdom so that he could return to India to marry a village girl from another caste and sentence his family to a life of suffering.

"Our Dawinder could have married whoever he wanted even after he came back," Kulwant Kaur said as she lifted a corner of her *dupatta* to wipe her eyes. "There were so many proposals. They were giving cars and fridges and washing machines and suitcases full of gold."

Neetu studied the marbled floor and willed the earth to split open so it could consume her the way she had watched it swallow the Goddess Sita in the latest televised version of the ancient Hindu epic poem *Ramayana*. She suddenly realized that as Goddess Sita had to endure a humiliating trial by fire to prove her fidelity, she would also have to do something drastic to prove her loyalty to her husband's family.

"My friend Varsha was saying my mummy still calls her," Neetu told the room full of Dawinder's relatives. As she spoke, she felt the cold stares stabbing her body. "She was telling Varsha, 'Beta, do you know where Neetu is? She didn't think about us even once. Now, why should we think about her?'" A long, uncomfortable silence fell over the room. In the stillness, the sounds of the street outside filled Kulwant Kaur's living room. A dog howled. Children shrieked and ran across into the fields. A clay oven sparked. Someone hummed the tune of a Punjabi rap song.

"Tell me one thing: What will happen when your baby comes?"

Bunty Singh turned to Dawinder to spare everyone the pain of the deepening silence. For long stretches over the past three years, since Dawinder had been deported back to India from the United Kingdom, he had assisted Bunty at his mobile service dealership. Dawinder rode his cousin's motorbike to roughly thirty-five small shops across the district each day to boost sales of mobile credit. He also helped out around the house to show his gratitude for the support his aunt's family extended to his parents.

"If you ran away for your own happiness," Bunty went on, "you should have also thought about how you are going to be safe and how you are going to keep your family safe. You need to change track, brother. You need to grow up. Think about things. Work harder." Bunty, a thick-set man with large, dull eyes, scolded in a voice barren of emotion, the kind of disdain to which Dawinder was overly sensitive. "Now, see, after you ran away and got married, what happened to your parents? Your mother got beaten up. They are living alone. They can't go home. I don't even want to call your mother and ask her how she is. You know why? Because I will get angry. I will not be able to control my anger. They are left there to die on the road, and you are staying here in luxury, eating and drinking to your heart's content. If you are alive, your hands and feet work, and still you can't look after your parents, what is your life worth?"

Bunty Singh said that he had called Dawinder's younger sister, Jasbir, recently. She confided that she had been having suicidal thoughts because her in-laws taunted and harassed her after Neetu and Dawinder eloped. "They tell her, 'You are dirty. Your brother ran away with a girl from another caste.' She says, 'I would rather die than live a life like this.' Which brother can tolerate his sister telling him that she would rather die?"

Dawinder began to heave to stop himself from crying in front of everyone. His eyes stung, and his throat went dry. After a while, Bunty Singh and Shanty Singh got up from the foam sofa, picked up their office satchels, and left for work. Dawinder wiped his face with a handkerchief, folded it, and slipped it back inside his pants pocket and followed his cousins out the door.

◆----◇----◆

Later that evening, when Dawinder returned home from work with his cousins, his sisters-in-law rushed to the door to collect their bags and offer them glasses of cold water. Dawinder looked through his sisters-in-law and into the house to see if Neetu was working in the kitchen or drying clothes out on the verandah.

The cousins washed their hands at the sink on the outside bathroom wall, and the sisters-in-law flitted around in a happy commotion, laying the dining table with hot rotis, pickle, and curd.

"Shall I serve you too if Neetu is still resting?" one sister-in-law asked Dawinder as he sat down at the dining table. When Dawinder replied that his wife was probably freshening up before she came downstairs to serve him dinner, a pitying smile spread across her face.

"Are you sure?" she asked him again a half hour later when Bunty Singh and Shanty Singh had wiped their mouths and stretched out in front of the evening television news. Just then Neetu appeared at the mouth of the spiral staircase, looking like she had been woken up by the voices downstairs. Her eyes were heavy with sleep, her hair was disheveled, and her kurta and pajama were creased. Dawinder told his sister-in-law he was still full from lunch and ran up to his room.

Neetu followed him upstairs, carrying a dinner plate. Dawinder was fuming. "Everywhere we go, everyone says the same thing!" he shouted. "Whether it's the Love Commandos. Whether it is here with Aunt Kulwant. They all say you are lazy. You sleep all day. You don't do any work. You don't care about anything. You don't care about anyone. Not even your own husband! Is everyone lying? The whole world is lying? Are you the only true one?"

"What did I do now?" Neetu said, fighting back tears. She wanted to explain that his aunt had allowed her to rest upstairs that afternoon to sleep off her first-trimester pains, and she had promised to wake up Neetu before Dawinder came home. But Neetu chose to stay quiet because she knew that Kulwant Kaur was probably listening to them with her ear pressed against their bedroom door.

In the absence of Dawinder's mother, Kulwant Kaur had taken it upon herself to train Neetu to become a good daughter-in-law. She demanded to be called Mummy, forbade Neetu from using a cell phone, and banned her from going upstairs to her room during the daytime because she believed naps made young wives lazy. "How come you don't write in your diary about how much we take care of you here?" Kulwant Kaur told Neetu one day after she had snuck up to her bedroom and gone through her personal belongings. "What more will we have to do to deserve some praise from the Great Neetu Rani?"

Late into the night, Neetu and Dawinder lay in bed separately, their faces turned away, awake with their own thoughts. Neetu thought about the tragic episode of the TV adaptation of *Ramayana* in which the Goddess Sita is abandoned by her husband because his kingdom refuses to accept her as a queen. When the early morning light slanted through the window, Dawinder looked at his wife and said tenderly. "Let's not fight," declaring the argument over.

◆┄┄◇┄┄➤

In the days after the attack on her mother-in-law, Neetu prayed regularly. In the brief time they had spent together, Neetu felt Sukhwinder Kaur's love pour over her like the first rain of the monsoon season. Whereas Kulwant Kaur would complain that Neetu did not know how to cook, Sukhwinder Kaur would patiently say that it was a matter of time before she learned. Then she would take her daughter-in-law's hand and teach her how to roll rotis as thin as handkerchiefs. She would squat on the bathroom floor and show her how to preserve the dye of new clothes when washing them. She would press her legs and pat her to sleep. "Beta, I'm teaching you all this so that no one can point fingers at you," Sukhwinder Kaur told Neetu. "But when we are in our own house, I will do everything. You will never have to worry about anything."

As for her own mother, Neetu felt only burning contempt. How was it possible for a mother to pick up a sickle and destroy her daughter's married life? How could her mother claim to love her the most of her three children? How could a mother sentence her own daughter to a lifetime of humiliation? How was Neetu supposed to allow herself to be showered in love from Dawinder's mother, a woman who had been beaten nearly to death because of her?

"I miss Mummy," Neetu told Dawinder the day Sukhwinder Kaur was discharged from the hospital. "When will she come here?"

"Soon," Dawinder answered with his eyes closed. For the first time in weeks, he looked relaxed, listening to Taylor Swift songs on the TV with his feet flung over the chair. For a while, Neetu sat on the sofa and watched him enjoy the music, his face growing soft. She asked him to play a Punjabi song that moved her to tears when they were apart, and suddenly an argument erupted between them over which song to play next. "I started crying in the room upstairs," she wrote in her diary. "I wanted to die. I felt as if there is no one in this world that is mine."

Ever since they moved in with Kulwant Kaur, they had fallen into an unfamiliar pattern of fighting and falling asleep without resolving the argument. At the shelter, they would toss and turn until the morning, until their anger melted, and then they confessed how much they loved each other.

Late some nights, Neetu went through Dawinder's text messages while he was asleep, even though she knew it would make him mad if he found out. She felt compelled to try to understand the workings of his mind.

Neetu came across this text message to a friend: "Mummy and Daddy are upset. My little sister is upset. Neetu is upset. Everyone is upset because of me. Why did I ever come back from England? What's the point of any of this?

"Love marriage = destroy life of everyone who belong to you."

Lately, Dawinder had become so distant, Neetu worried whether he would ever return to her. He would answer her with nods. He would suddenly stop listening when she complained about her pregnancy pains or a nightmare that had woken her up. He would allow Kulwant Kaur and her daughters-in-law to scold her about little things. He would eat dinner without asking if she was hungry, and he would fall asleep before she came upstairs.

When Neetu tried to remember that he was the same man who had only months earlier performed sit-ups in a room full of people at the Love Commandos shelter just to make her smile, she felt a tight-ness spread across her chest. Remembering happy moments brought its own kind of strange sadness.

◆·····◇·····▶

Early one morning, Dawinder shook Neetu awake and asked her to bring him a glass of warm milk for his headache. Since she had fallen asleep in a thin, low-cut blouse and forgotten to put a robe under her pillow, Dawinder tossed his shirt to her and asked her to change into it before going downstairs to the kitchen.

"How many times have I told you not to wear these kinds of tops?" he said to her as she changed into his shirt.

"I forgot," she muttered sleepily.

"You can do whatever you want when we move into our own house. Wear your underwear and walk around. No one will say a word."

Neetu dismissed Dawinder's harsh comments as a symptom of his headache and went downstairs to bring the milk. When she re-turned to the room, she saw him tearing her camisole blouse into shreds. "Use this to mop the floor," he sneered, tossing the torn pieces across the room.

"Why would you do that?" Neetu shouted as she burst into tears. She ran into the bathroom and locked herself in to cry, and Dawinder realized he had gone too far. After a while, when the door did not open, he pressed his ear against it. "I'm sorry," he said to the door. "I'll buy you a new top."

"No," she answered. "I won't wear anything you buy me."

"Please, I'll buy it today," he said. "Please, please, please. I hate fighting with you."

There was silence from the bathroom.

"Okay, I know what to do," Dawinder said as he clapped his hands. "Now you will *have* to forgive me." For the first time in weeks, his voice sounded familiar to Neetu.

Dawinder took off his shirt, bit a corner of it, and tore it in two. Neetu unlocked the bathroom door to peep outside when she heard the ripping of fabric. "What a mad husband I have!" She burst out laughing as she picked up the torn pieces of his shirt and sat down to stitch them back together.

❖

The next day, Neetu slept in until noon, and in the hours that followed, she hardly moved. During the first trimester of her pregnancy, she had been vomiting whatever Kulwant Kaur and her daughters-in-law cooked at home, so Dawinder took the day off from work to take care of her. He made her a bowl of instant noodles and brought it to bed. Later in the afternoon, when she finally padded downstairs, still in her pajamas, he fed her a bowl of *kheer*, a sweet rice pudding, with his own hands.

"Look at this boy," Kulwant Kaur said scornfully from across the room. "What will my daughters-in-law expect from my sons if they see a man sitting at home and feeding his wife?"

Dawinder laughed and promised to feed whoever was hungry. He was determined to let nothing dampen his spirits today after news arrived that his parents had left Kakheri for good and were on their way to join them at Kulwant Kaur's house. Within weeks, the four of them would move into their own house down the lane with the money they had earned from selling their fields in the village, and they would finally start their lives again.

At the dining table, Neetu put her head on Dawinder's shoulder, he put his arm around her, and they called the Love Commandos. Lately, they had become nostalgic about the shelter and its simplifying retreat from the brutality of real life. "Have any new couples come?" they wanted to know. Neetu had taken to calling the stay at the shelter their "honeymoon."

Mohammad Arif Dosani and Monika Ingle, a Muslim and
Hindu couple from the western Indian state of Maharashtra, find
themselves swept up in a political conspiracy known as love jihad,
a Hindu nationalist narrative stoked by Prime Minister Narendra
Modi's ruling party that plays on dark fears that Muslims lure
Hindu women into marriage to water down the Hindu majority.

Monika thinks her sister secretly harbors feelings for Arif
and tips off the Bajrang Dal, a militant Hindutva outfit. After
midnight, men wielding swords barge into Hasanbagh, to attack
Arif's family. Months later, Monika gives birth to their daughter.

Chapter 15

Objects in the Mirror

One afternoon in April 2018, Monika Ingle was in one of her whimsical moods, glancing sidelong in a shaving mirror to inspect her face for new blemishes, determined to go through the rest of her day flicking away the annoyances buzzing around her. The first time she saw this one-room flat on the second floor of a building that resembled an open mouth with rotting teeth, two lanes away from Arif's parents' house in Basmath, a violent itch started at her toes and crawled up to her neck, with the growing suspicion that a rodent infestation had made the accommodation affordable. Monika had forced a display of satisfaction, since the frustration of living with her in-laws outweighed the inconveniences of living on her own. But after the rent was handed over to the landlord in a creased plastic bag and added to the loan amount to be repaid by Arif, his grandmother Momina announced that she would move in with her for safety.

Momina, a large woman with the face of a marmalade cat, now sat across the room in a cheap cotton nightgown. She flared her nostrils to emphasize that she was waiting for Monika to help her down the stairs to a plastic chair under the neem tree, where she would spend the rest of the afternoon watching the neighborhood swirl around her. These days, Monika was capable of acting out small irritations into dramatic rages. If the secondhand air cooler stopped working, for instance, she would hurl her slipper at it and sit down to cry. Or if Arif's mother brought another watery curry of dill and spinach leaves, telling her it would help her lactate, she would let out a brief shriek and sit down to cry again. So Momina preferred to wait for Monika to discern the meaning of her trembling nostrils.

"Where is the Queen of Nagpur?" a voice boomed above the rumble of the cooler.

Monika's face suddenly lit up. Tabu Pathan, a young woman who lived one floor below, was standing at the door, hair tossed to the side, butterfly clip dangling from her grin. Tabu's clever eyes flickered with audacity in a neighborhood where it was impossible for a woman to step out of her home without a burka and make it to the end of the lane without succumbing to the gunfire of taunts. She took up more space than her wiry body consumed, she was careless about how she sat, and she was skilled at peppering her rants with English cuss words. Her energy spread like a conquering fire wherever she went, and she seemed to Monika like the kind of girl who was meant for a bigger and better place—perhaps a city like Mumbai—just like her.

A year had passed since Tabu's fourth sister married. Because this placed her next in line, she was required to drop out of college and prepare for marriage. In addition to learning how to cook and run a household, the training included unlearning everything she read in magazines or saw on television by attending Quran class to fill her mind with holy thoughts. The new lessons were expected to be put to use by resisting the temptation to mouth off to elders or swear at children.

That afternoon, Tabu had ditched her youngest sister in Quran class and snuck up to chat with Monika.

"I want to run away, *yaar*," Tabu sighed, standing in a puddle of her burka. "Life is so boring here."

"No, no, you shouldn't run away," Monika said. "It's very bad to do that." How she enjoyed saying the words.

"Look who's talking!" Tabu said, laughing.

"I'm telling you," Monika said, "you can't trust these boys of today."

"But you trusted a boy and ran away?"

"Arif is different," she said with a smile. "He's a class apart."

"Who says I'm running with a boy?" Tabu slapped her knee. "I'll run alone."

"How can you do that?" Monika asked. "Where will you go?"

"Somewhere far away," she said. "Where no one pokes their nose in your business."

Talking to Tabu felt like meeting a younger version of her sister, Bhagyashri. During those afternoons, Monika could lift her mood by recounting memories of Nagpur with someone who understood the suffocation of being trapped in a place too small for them. In these retellings of her old life, everything shone and sparkled, and it became possible to forget that, despite being in a marriage, she and Arif were now each only one half of a couple, splintered across miles and worlds because of his ambition to become a police constable.

◆┄┄◇┄┄➤

One evening Monika sat cross-legged on the floor, holding her two-month-old baby, Alina, to her breast. She scrolled through a phone to look at old photos with one hand and balanced a second phone to her ear to talk to Arif. Momina lay on the kitchen floor, her face turned away, starting a new cycle of prayer.

"Arif, what are you doing? You're sending all the bad photos," she grumbled. "Send the one of me wearing my white dress with sunglasses. And the one in my black top where I am wearing a sun hat."

"Madam," he said, "I am washing clothes."

On any other day, Arif would have been happy to indulge Monika because hearing her voice fill up with sudden happiness at the vision of herself as a young girl with her whole life ahead of her was always more pleasant than listening to her complain about his family. But today he was too tired to play along. He had woken at four in the morning, grabbed his running shoes, and dashed out of his dorm room, but he had reached the training grounds three minutes late. He paid for it with a punishment of three more laps of the scorching earth with a heavy rifle slung across his shoulder. Later that afternoon, in the fifteen-minute break after the law and civics lecture, he had skipped lunch to pray and comfort his father about a new financial crisis he had landed himself in. After another bootcamp training, he had finally managed to get his hands on a cup of tea, but a supervisor had walked into the canteen to instruct him to prune eight peepul trees before sunset. Now he was running a fever and staring at a load of unfinished laundry, but his wife wanted to see a photo of herself lounging in the wave pool at an amusement park.

"What did you eat today?" Arif asked to change the topic.

"Spinach and dill curry," she said, a shiver of disgust shooting through her body. "Why does your mother keep tormenting me with spinach and dill?"

"Your husband is washing his own clothes. Your mother-in-law is feeding you," Arif said. "And you are the one complaining?"

◆——◇——➤

Early on a Sunday morning, Arif's childhood friend Khaled arrived at Monika's door and told her to get ready. Khaled was dressed neatly, with his hair parted to the side and a gold-plated pen that he wore only for special occasions poking out of his shirt pocket. He had learned early in life, after losing his leg to polio, to always present himself as a formal, no-nonsense kind of man because he knew how quickly a cripple who opened himself to laughter became the butt of the joke. But today a glimmer of a smile in his eyes matched the twinkle of his pen.

Since Arif left for training six months earlier, Khaled had taken it upon himself to look after his friend's wife. Before leaving for work at a copy shop, where his job was to help villagers apply for government identification cards, he dropped by Monika's house to ask if she needed groceries or medicines, and returned in the evening with her supplies. Monika would listen for the tap of Khaled's bamboo crutch against the metal ladder leading to her flat and begin preparing a cup of a tea.

"Are we really going to Latur?" she asked excitedly.

Monika cleared the bed for Khaled to sit down, plopped baby Alina in his lap, and ran to the bathroom to change into her best hand-embroidered *salwar kameez* for the second meeting with her husband in a half year. She dabbed a fistful of talcum powder on her face, rimmed her eyes with kohl, smudged a dollop of lipstick on her cheeks, and wore a floral hijab instead of her usual black burka. During the five-hour trip by taxi, Monika laughed, clapped, sang songs, and tickled her baby's toes.

When Arif walked into the truck-stop food stall they were waiting in, he barged in like a storm, rolling his sleeves, his face screwed up in a scowl, eyes vacant. "You reached here and didn't even bother to call Papa to inform him that you arrived safely?" he said in a voice empty of affection.

"I was going to call him," Monika muttered.

Watching Arif stand around indifferently, showing Khaled photos of himself with new guns, talking about the movies he had been watching, and taking long sips of soda, instead of holding the baby he had seen three times since her birth, Monika felt a dam breaking inside her. Her face burned with embarrassment, and she blinked furiously to keep her tears from falling.

When it finally dawned on Arif that his wife was throwing a quiet tantrum because she had started pretending not to hear him, he took her aside. "What did I do?" he asked. "I'm sorry that I am such a big idiot."

Monika, ready to scream, wanted to count for him all the ways in which he had let her down and make him realize how much he had to be grateful for, but she plopped down in the chair with a whimper. "A very, very, very, very big idiot," she agreed.

◆┄┄◇┄┄▶

Summer came and went in Basmath. Monsoon clouds hovered overhead with urgency but passed without breaking. When winter finally arrived, Monika pushed open the window to feel the cool breeze on her face, but suddenly her throat felt raw, and her head felt like it was about to shatter. By night, her eyes had turned into craters, and her body was smoldering. A street-corner doctor prescribed medicines to bring down the fever and suggested a diet of glucose biscuits dunked in water, but two weeks later, the illness still lingered.

Arif convinced Monika to move back in with his parents so that his mother could cook and look after baby Alina. Monika's days passed in a blur of ferrying endless rounds of tea to Tabssum with what felt like only half her usual strength, until one day she was too weak to answer her husband's call to complain about his mother. Arif, deciding that this was a disease with only one cure, arranged for Monika to move to Nagpur to live with his aunt Akida until his police training wrapped up three months later.

When Monika stepped off the bus in Nagpur, hollow cheeked and coughing, she took a deep breath to savor her city for the first time in a year. She tasted a mouthful of dust and noticed how the roads looked wider, the buildings looked taller, and the people looked happier. By the time her rickshaw hobbled into Hasanbagh, where she would live with Aunt Akida, instead of turning home to her parents' house, her excitement had turned into dread.

As days passed, Monika waited for cracks to appear in Akida's kindness, but over time, her suspicions melted away, and she came to believe that Akida's heart was really as large and forgiving as everyone said. Finally, true to Arif's prediction, Monika started to feel more and more like herself. Slowly, the color returned to her face, and a sharpness came back to her tongue. But then the familiar laments began.

The fact that she was so close but still so far from her parents struck her in waves. Every time she called a cousin to reminisce and collect a snatch of news about her family, she felt a surge of sudden energy, like she was missing a train. She heard that her sister, Bhagyashri, was selected for police training. Her brother, Amit, was offered a full-time role as a high school roller skating teacher. Her father Shridhar's cotton mattress business had prospered so much since she left that the family had moved into a new house down the lane with eight big rooms. The rooms were bright, the floors were tiled, and big, beautiful paintings dressed the walls.

The afternoon that photos of a family function in the new house arrived, Monika had to tear her eyes away from the screen because the brightness made them water. The destitution of the past year had shrunk the mental reserves of her memories of her family, and now, suddenly seeing her parents in brocade and silk, laughing with all their teeth, it occurred to her that they were no longer mourning for her. She pinched the screen to zoom in and out of Bhagyashri, studying her white sundress, the delicate gold earrings that fell like little bells, eyes flecked with golden shimmer, hair sculpted into little ringlets, and she became surer than ever that her sister had finally succeeded in sucking up all of her family's love.

The next evening, Monika threw on her burka, borrowed Jikar's motorbike, and sped toward her parents' house. As she slithered onto the quiet lane of her childhood, past the row of identical low-rise buildings, beyond the municipal school where little girls in plaits emerged in pairs, toward the small temple where she mumbled all her grievances as a schoolgirl, she felt as if she were touring an open-air museum of loss.

Monika slowed down at the double-door gate of the new house,

craned her neck, stretched her spine, and squinted to look for shadows
of her family. The main door to the house was bolted from inside,
and the balcony was empty, so she closed her eyes to imagine what
she might have seen. At this time, her mother would be scampering
around the kitchen to get dinner ready before hunger-induced tempers flared. Her father would be on a lace-trimmed couch in front of
the TV, lamenting the decline of Hindi entertainment. Her brother
would be standing behind him performing acrobatics to make the
remote work.

At a distance, Monika noticed her sister's pearl-white scooter
and walked her bike closer, heart thumping, to see if the front panel
still had the sticker that said "Monika" in silver cursive lettering.
When the scooter was bought years earlier, her father had distributed sweets, her mother had tied a holy thread for protection from
accidents and theft, and Monika had teared up watching her sister
fix a sticker of her name. Despite the events of the past year, the
sticker was still there, unscratched, unvandalized, unharmed. So
much happiness filled Monika's heart in that moment that it was
starting to ache.

At home in Hasanbagh, her bones cracked like potato chips from
exhaustion, but she could not rest. Night after night, she lay awake
with her thoughts. "The government has not levied any tax on
dreaming and hoping for good things," her husband told her on the
phone. It irritated Monika that Arif used her vulnerability to lecture
her. "But please remember that your parents are still very angry, and
people do bad things when they are angry."

Still, for the next weeks, Monika borrowed Jikar's motorbike,
choosing a new time to visit every day, desperately wishing for a
familiar face, but she returned wearing the same harrowed look

of disappointment. When she looked at baby Alina's face, she saw her father's gentle smile, the way her dimples dinged deep into her cheeks, and a dull ache throbbed inside her at the thought of her daughter growing up without his affection.

One evening, Monika waited at a traffic light at rush hour, watching tides of office workers surging out of big buildings, laptop bags slung across shoulders, umbrellas pressed under elbows, little tiffin boxes dangling, when her gaze wandered to a van that had paused beside her. Shridhar was in the driver's seat. She stared ravenously into her father's face, unsure if her mind was playing tricks again, but he must have been real, because he felt her eyes on him and turned toward her.

Then she saw his face burn with disgust, the light turned green, and he drove away, leaving her with a silence that was louder than the din of a city emptying out for the night.

"He didn't see me, but I saw how his face changed the moment he saw a burka," she told Arif on the phone that night. "Because it must have brought up painful memories about me."

"It's okay," he told her. "Take this and cherish it." Arif reminded her that four months had passed since she returned to Nagpur and that they were moving to Mumbai soon. In two days, she would leave for Basmath to gather their belongings from his parents' house.

The day before her bus to Basmath, Monika decided to drive past her parents' house one last time. This final attempt at catching a glimpse of her family was certain to be futile, as it had been countless times before, so she decided to leave her burka at home.

When she turned in to Reshimbagh, the only time she was prepared to leave the city with nothing, her family materialized one by one. Shridhar and Ranjana were at the gate; her father's arm hung fraternally around her mother. They had probably wandered outside after evening tea for fresh air, because they were still in their home clothes: Shridhar in his Bermuda shorts, and Ranjana in her red and yellow cotton sari. Monika dashed past them without making eye contact, took a turn at the mouth of the lane, and returned for a second glimpse. By then, Amit had joined his parents outside, and she was sure he had cracked a joke because her mother was making the face she made whenever she suppressed an irresistible urge to laugh.

Monika came back for a third glimpse, and just as she dreamily breezed past them one last time with large, moist eyes, she heard a squeal: "Mona *didi!*" Elder sister. "Is it you?" The neighbor's young daughter had recognized her. The voice was so shrill and so close that she felt it sprang from her own heart, and, in the moment, not knowing what else to do, she slammed the accelerator, tearing through the narrow lanes of her childhood with the fright of hunted prey. She was grateful for her instinct because Amit was behind her, following on his motorbike, barreling toward her, screaming her name. Somehow, despite the tears stinging her eyes, Monika managed to keep her focus on the road, maneuvering her motorbike through meandering lanes whose paths she had forgotten, and by some miracle, she lost her brother before turning into Hasanbagh.

When she walked into Akida's house, she threw her purse to the floor, grabbed baby Alina, and frantically kissed her everywhere. Arif's aunt teared up watching her from the kitchen. She did not need to ask what happened.

◆⋯⋯◇⋯⋯➤

The next morning, as Monika set out from Nagpur, she watched the city grow smaller and smaller through the battered window of the state transport bus. Relief fell on her like a warm blanket and lulled her into a deep sleep. When her eyes opened as the bus slowed to a crawl in Basmath, baby Alina still asleep at her chest, she scanned the faces outside her window and saw Khaled jogging alongside the bus, waving happily.

"So?" he said as she loaded her duffle bag into the rickshaw. "Happy to be home?"

Arriving at a meaning of home had become an exercise in slow recovery. Until the day before, home was Nagpur, where she had bathed in the affection of her family, where her mother taught herself recipes of fancy dishes Monika craved, where her father called her favorite Hindi radio station hundreds of times just to see her squeal with joy at hearing a surprise song dedication on her birthday. Now that city felt like a scar on which a scab was forming very slowly and painfully. The thought of losing Arif and baby Alina, flashing and blinking before her eyes as she tore through the city, not knowing what Amit might have done if he had managed to get a hold of her, and the possibility that her brother might have dragged her to Reshimbagh, locked her up, and never allowed her to see her daughter again had shaken and rearranged Monika's understanding of home. She had ached so long to regain her family's love that she had not been able to see that what she really wished for now was nothing except to be with Arif and Alina. When she thought of home now, she imagined a simple room somewhere in Mumbai, where she would finally start a new life.

The process of grieving her old home and allowing memories to dwell only in memories had in some ways relaxed something inside her. At lunch, when Arif's mother, Tabssum, slapped another bowl of dill and spinach curry before her, it made her laugh. She lay her head in Arif's grandmother Momina's lap and asked to hear verses from the Quran about forgiveness.

Weeks later, Tabu, the neighbor from two floors down, called with the news that her wedding had been arranged with a cleric who ran a religious school in the village. "Are you happy?" Monika asked.

"I think you know this better than me," Tabu answered bitterly. "A girl's happiness depends on how fast she adjusts to her husband and in-laws."

Chapter 16

Sorry, Wrong Number

In August 2018 Mohammad Arif Dosani arrived in Mumbai to start his job as a police constable. After midnight, when the train clanked into the Chhatrapati Shivaji Terminus, a cloud of golden light suspended in darkness, Arif clenched his eyes shut to slow the moment: a dream he had nourished with sacrifices for half his life was coming true. When he opened his eyes, he was inside the golden cloud, in the center of a mass of humanity swirling so fast that he felt himself tumbling like laundry inside a washing machine, until the crowds spat him out into the city, shirt crumpled, hair ruffled, drenched in sweat.

"Welcome to Mumbai, bro!" a voice called out from behind, and Arif's cousin Arbaz jumped off a parapet of the ancient terminal building. Arbaz, a splay-footed twenty-year-old with mischievous eyes, had run away from home when he was still a boy with a mouth full of missing teeth.

"What's up, bro?" Arif grinned, the English words passing through his rustic soul like a remix song out of a harmonium.

Over the hardscrabble years in the city, Arbaz had somehow found his way into the gig economy of Hindi movies as a light and sound production assistant, living in a suspended state of feast or famine, debauchery or destitution, good humor or insolence. Since he was just coming off a high of four months of continuous work, and his spirits were still buoyant, he had invited Arif to stay with him until he found a place of his own. As the cousins walked toward the local railway station to take another train to the northern suburbs, Arbaz boasted about movie stars who turned down big projects if it became known to them that he was not on the set. Arif glanced at his cousin's cell phone, a rolling gallery of selfies with moderately famous people, and recoiled in mock surprise at every swipe even though he had a hard time recognizing the faces.

Beyond the blizzard of traffic and the fortress of towering buildings, Arif could make out the Arabian Sea. Lovers sat pressed up against each other on the promenade, a salty breeze on their tongues, making promises. A tea boy cruised on his cycle, steel tumbler rattling behind, swinging the handlebar from side to side, singing his heart out. Taxi drivers parked their cars at the seaside, flung their legs out of windows, and slept like kings. Arif decided that he would bring Monika here when she came to the city to show her how, from where he was standing, enormous buildings looked like dollhouses, and the rich people inside them looked like string-puppets.

◆┄┄◆┄┄▶

In the weeks before leaving for Mumbai, Arif had started watching the popular crime series *Sacred Games* and daydreaming about landing an assignment like the hero, an honest policeman named Sartaj Singh, who gets a tip from a fabled gangster about a plot to wipe out the city of Mumbai. Inspector Singh thrashes through squalid lanes of the undercity, dodges bullets, jumps out of third-floor windows, befriends prostitutes, and joins a cult to untangle the links between organized crime and political leadership, turning into the only man who can save the city from nuclear attack. Watching the show filled Arif with a frenzy of adventure and discovery. This was the kind of work he was cut out for: *kadak*. Hard-core.

But with his first posting, it became clear that in real life, a police job was the kind of work that put a man in danger of dying not from a bullet but from excruciating boredom. He was assigned to the bungalow of a ninety-seven-year-old Hindi film actor who was granted police protection over a property dispute against a builder with a colorful criminal record. For twelve hours every day, Arif sat by the metal gate, holding a rifle in his lap like a sleeping baby. At eleven every morning, when the actor's seventy-five-year-old wife woke from her sleep and hobbled downstairs to breathe the fresh air in her garden, Arif stood up with half his body to pay his respects. The rest of the day went by drinking tea, making small talk with the boy who sold him the tea, and reading the same newspaper over and over until he could narrate the headlines with his eyes closed. By the end of the first week, he started leaving his watch at home, because the more he looked at it, the slower it moved.

"Ten years ago, our police force was the best in the whole world," Arif told Arbaz over dinner one night. "If a crime was about to happen, they would come to know three hours before. Two cops could take down two hundred criminals in their sleep. If a cop walked on the road, the crowd would part in fear."

"And now?" Arbaz sneered. The answer was already written on his cousin's face, but hearing it would be even more satisfying.

"At least it's not like the film line—earning like a hero today and a zero tomorrow," Arif retorted.

To keep his optimism intact, Arif tried to extract every small thrill from the privileges granted by his khaki uniform. For instance, free public transport. Every morning on his way to work, Arif boarded one bus, jumped off at a red light, and hopped onto another bus locked in traffic ahead. "You could be the richest person in Mumbai, but you still have to sit in traffic," Arif became fond of telling Monika on the phone. "Only a policeman can get to a place in half the time." Monika, who was in Basmath to gather their things, greedily consumed every snatch of information Arif shared about the new city. In her diary, she kept a tally of the days that were passing by, waiting for her husband to send her a train ticket to Mumbai. When Arif first left for Mumbai, Alina had begun learning to crawl. Now she was running everywhere.

In Mumbai, Arif's next posting was more exciting. It was still protection duty but at the home of a political family that ruled a Hindu-nationalist party and had been in power for as long as Arif had been alive. At the height of his popularity, the party's patriarch, who wore saffron robes and tinted sunglasses, clamored against a moving target of outsiders who flocked to Mumbai and cornered jobs, excluding native Maharashtrians from opportunities in their booming city. The Hindus born in Mumbai's home state, he said, were "sons of the soil." First, he blamed the South Indians. Then, the Gujaratis, migrants from a neighboring state on India's west coast. Movie actors who came from out of state. A painter who depicted Hindu deities in the nude. Writers and journalists. North Indians.

Somewhere on his long list of enemies were also Muslims, against whom he had been accused of inciting a pogrom when Arif was still a baby. But that was a detail that seemed irrelevant to be hung up over to Arif, since in the final years of the patriarch's life, before his death in 2012, the leader had softened toward Muslims, his spectacular contempt fizzling into weak insults such as calling the community antinational and asking Muslims to go to Pakistan.

After the patriarch's death, the party was inherited by his son, who Arif thought was a slumbering shadow of his father. Now it was Arif's job to protect him as part of a team of seventy-five officers. Before his death, the patriarch had cast himself as a modern-day Chhatrapati Shivaji Maharaj, the seventeenth-century Hindu warrior king whose ragtag guerrilla army resisted invasion from the formidable Mughal Empire. Arif had heard that somewhere inside the mansion, there was still a monitor lizard, the kind Shivaji was said to have trained to assist in scaling cliffs and forts in battle, but he never got to see it. He spent his days in a lawn chair behind a sandbag bunker at the gate, either listening to stories of glory days from party workers who streamed in and out of the mansion or filling his time playing an endless game of guessing which rich and famous personality had arrived to settle important business with the powerful people inside. On the phone, he would describe to Monika how the big men and women of the city kicked off their shoes and sandals at the gate and tiptoed inside barefoot, like pilgrims.

Slowly, Arif started suspecting that beneath the mythology of Mumbai's modernity were the same festering Hindu-Muslim grievances that had shaped his life in Nagpur and Basmath. As a precaution, whenever someone asked about his personal life, he never let it slip that his wife had once been Hindu.

"It's better to keep quiet," Arif told Monika. "They should not have something in their heart against me. That I took a girl from their religion. Because that is bound to hurt."

"You are right," his wife agreed.

"This hatred between Hindus and Muslims," he said. "It divided India into India and Pakistan."

✦┈┈◇┈┈✦

After the Diwali festival of lights in November, Monika arrived in Mumbai. Arif had finally put down the deposit for a room two buildings away from Arbaz's home, in a safe part of the Teghi Masjid area in the northern suburb of Malvani. From the look of it, the chawl was exactly like Hasanbagh, with its rivers of sewer sludge, cramped chicken shops, smoldering cooking fires, and decomposing rat carcasses. At first glance, Monika feared that Nagpur's slum huts had multiplied, sprawled, and crept all the way to Mumbai. But the feel of this place was nothing like the villages. Across the street, in a small open field, she saw a little girl, still in her school uniform, cursing at a group of boys for cheating her out of her turn to bat in a game of cricket. Monika's face lit up as she watched the girl, bristling with rage, showcase an impressive selection of expletives. And Monika finally found the word she was searching for: this place was *bindaas*. Carefree. It was the right place to raise Alina, so that she could grow into a woman who would not allow her voice to be stifled.

Their new house was a single room on the mezzanine floor of a building that looked like it was standing entirely on willpower. In a city that was so noisy that it often drowned out the voice of one's own thoughts, Arif told her, this was the only place he found with *sukoon*.

Tranquility. As he flung open the window, which looked out upon a mahogany tree, Arif explained that the blast of dust that came here was cooler than the air in the more expensive apartments downstairs.

"The fridge will come here," Monika responded. "And a TV up here."

"Yes, madam." He nodded.

"And a Wi-Fi router also," she added.

As soon as she saw it, Monika settled into her new home with a peace that had evaded her in all the temporary addresses that came before it. In her flat in Basmath, she had taken a ballpoint pen and etched "Arif Mona" with all her strength into the wooden door, but in this home, she felt no need to claim it, since it already felt like her own. Here she could sleep in till midday, bake cakes in a pressure cooker, try on her dungarees, and paint her lips bright red.

Whenever she felt lonely, she would call the landlady of the flat, the owner of a hair salon down the road, who seemed nicer than she should have been, given her flip-top perm and manicured nails. The landlady would come over with fried rice and a chicken leg or a box of pineapple pastries, and they would talk for hours. When they had exhausted all topics, they would stretch out on the floor and listen to songs from the new movie *Gully Boy*, laughing at the sight of baby Alina bursting into little involuntary dances.

This new film was about a lower-middle-class Muslim boy from a slum that looked exactly like their own, who had turned his rage at the systems rigged against him into rap music. One evening, watching Alina chant the movie's powerful anthem, "Apna Time Ayega"—"Our Time Will Come"—bobbing her head, scowling, windmilling her arms, Monika dissolved into a fit of uncontrollable laughter, and in the hysteria, she realized later, she was also crying.

"Doesn't Alina remind you of Bhaga?" She turned to her husband in tears.

"Same to same," he said. Arif looked at Alina, who was splayed in front of a pack of biscuits, a cheeky grin spreading across her face. "Please forgive me," Arif said with hands folded to the toddler, and Monika shrieked with a renewed burst of laughter. "I know I ran away with your sweet Mona. But please, my head is bowed, I am begging you. Have some mercy."

On New Year's Eve 2018, Arif was working through the night, patrolling Marwe Beach for illegal possession of alcohol, and Monika was stuck at home without anything good to watch on TV, growing irritated that the Wi-Fi router had still not been installed.

In the weeks since she arrived in the city, Arif's police duty kept him away for longer and longer stretches, leaving him too tired to take her to the places he talked about so much. Monika had started feeling herself weakening with loneliness, a void she had concluded could be filled with an internet connection.

All those years since their marriage, she had wished for nothing but freedom from Arif's family, but now that they were away and her mind had finally been emptied of the daily bickering that occupied it, it was somehow filled with a haunting silence. She tried to shatter the quiet by immersing herself in an endless loop of daily soaps, attempting to invest herself in the lives of imaginary tycoons and distressed daughters-in-law, but after a while, those voices were drowned out too.

To jolt herself out of her dead skin, she made a mental note of all the ways that Arif's family had deprived her. She thought about how they had not hosted a wedding reception after she came to their home as a newlywed. Not even a single wedding gift. A simple gold chain cost close to nothing. The least her mother-in-law could have done was to stitch her a brocade blouse and skirt. And they had not even given baby Alina as much as a dress from their own clothes shop. "What kind of people are these?" she muttered to feel like herself again. "God only knows."

When Arif returned home from work, Monika asked how the rich people of the city had brought in the new year. He described a beach rave where people got high on drugs and danced like they were possessed by a peculiar demon who did not like songs with words. It was the strangest thing to watch, he said, to see them shake their arms and legs without their lips having anything to hum.

"What about the Wi-Fi?" she interrupted him. "I got so bored at home when you were out at the party."

"I wasn't at a party," he said. "I was at work."

"It sounds like a party."

"When will you learn to be happy with what you have?" he said and threw his towel to the floor.

"How many times have I told you to get it?" she said. "You keep saying you will get it, but it never comes."

Arif advised her to pray instead of complain, because this month, too, the last rupee they had managed to save after paying rent, electricity, water, and grocery bills had gone straight toward the loans that had tided them over during their elopement.

Days after his lecture on saving money, Arif took another loan to buy children's clothes to stock his father's shop in Basmath. Monika wanted to look him in the eye and tell him that she was not stupid. "What about my Wi-Fi?" she wanted to scream. "Will you always deprive us for them? What about my Wi-Fi? Where is it?" But once again she found herself flopping down on the bed with a sniffle and packing their bags to travel to the village to deliver the goods.

When they arrived at Arif's parents' home, Bashir swept away the bulging plastic bags of pinafores, frocks, shorts, and pants, and fished out a pink button-down shirt and put it on Alina. Monika had wanted to always see her daughter in shorts and pants, never a frock, because she wanted so badly for her to enjoy her days of carefree abandon before her body developed and became a prison sentence. Even before Monika had a chance to admire her daughter wearing new clothes for the first time in an eternity, she heard Arif's sister Shireen's voice, thwacking like a sledgehammer.

"A new top from the new stock?" Monika's sister-in-law said, saying without saying that Arif and Monika should pay for the top. Monika looked at Arif, standing like a mute, an awkward smile spreading across his face, leaving his sister's insult dangling in the air.

Throughout the two-week trip to the village, it was the rare day that passed without an argument sucking the air out of the room. When Monika whined while watching Tabssum give Alina a bath, tossing the baby over her shoulder like dirty laundry and splashing water across her crying face, Arif's mother suddenly started beating her chest and crying that her blue-blooded daughter-in-law did not think she was good enough to bathe a baby. When Monika asked Shireen for Arif's phone so that she could soothe Alina with her favorite songs, the teenager stomped out to complain that Monika had snatched the phone from her hand.

Arif's mother promptly burst through the door. "Who are you to snatch the phone? That phone is her brother's property."

"I didn't snatch it," Monika said. "Alina was crying for the phone."

"What kind of manners are these?" Tabssum said. "Is this how you were taught to talk to elders?"

◆┄┄◇┄┄◆

After the trip to the village, Monika started referring to Bashir and Tabssum as "Alina's grandfather" and "Alina's grandmother" instead of "Mummy" and "Papa" to show that she had removed herself from her husband's family. When Arif dialed them on video call, and they appeared on the screen with smiling faces, telling Monika that they missed her, she smiled and slunk out of the frame.

As time passed, she lost interest in everything that had once made her happy. The TV blared all day long, but Monika didn't know what was happening in her favorite shows because she had stopped listening. Her dungarees and red lipstick stayed bundled up on the shelf because she no longer dreamed of Arif taking her out. When Arif said that he didn't want to send Alina to school because it was too expensive, she nodded. In the mirror, a woman who looked like a shadow of herself stared back, skeletal, scattered hair, swollen eyes. She nurtured no expectations that someone would step into the door, shake her, and tell her that everything would be fine.

"In three-hour-long films, we only see what happens until a boy and girl fall in love and get married," Arif told Khaled on the phone one evening. "But what happens after? Who is feeding who? The girl will say two morsels are enough, but two morsels can never be someone's dream for long. As days pass, desires get bigger and bigger." For the first time in their two-decade friendship, Khaled had no advice for Arif.

One afternoon, Arif decided that he had to do something about his wife's frequent sad moods. He had the idea of calling her father, pretending to be a credit card salesman, in a foolproof plan to breathe life into his wife. Surely, the sound of Shridhar's voice would pull her out of this withering mess she had made of herself.

"Good morning, sir," Arif said in his singsong English-speaking delivery. "Do you require a credit card?"

"Sorry," her father snapped. "Wrong number."

A high-pitched pulsating beep filled the silence in Arif and Monika's home. Experiment over. Monika rose to serve dinner, and the family of three ate leftover dal and rice in silence once again. The next day, Arif came home with a new Wi-Fi router to dissipate the many kinds of thunders that was his wife's silence.

Arif's latest posting was inside the Aarey Milk Colony, a settlement of tribal hamlets at the boundary of the largest forest reserve in the city, to keep an eye on troublemakers who looked to sneak into the national park's restricted areas in order to spot leopards. Arif spent his days sitting among mango trees, beneath passing clouds, listening for mynahs and bulbuls and teaching two pariah dogs, Champa and Chameli, to shake hands. At dusk, after the city swallowed the sun, a blue mist rose, and a hush descended over the forest. Some constables found the silence and its deep darkness eerie, but to Arif it was clarifying.

One evening, sitting on his sleeping mat in the dingy police station in the forest, rummaging through his backpack for cotton earplugs to prevent centipedes from crawling inside his brain, it occurred to him that he had arrived at the final stop of his ambitions. In the mad dash to catch the train hurtling toward his bright future, he had forgotten to see where it was going. The towns that had flashed past his window, he could now see, were lost opportunities—the privilege of seeing pride in his father's eyes, the joy of watching Alina take her first steps, the freedom to tell Monika he would not leave her again. What he had earned so far—the khaki uniform on his back and the honor and stability that came with it—were enough for him. He now longed to go back home.

"Let's go back to Basmath," he told Monika.

"Okay." She nodded.

"I'll take a transfer," he explained.

She nodded again.

Arif had expected a big fight. At least an argument. Her lingering silence was proof that they were drifting. It was as if a ghost had materialized between them, a long and haunting presence that had taken them so far away from each other, they could no longer hear each other's voices.

One morning Arif woke to the sound of Monika talking on the phone. "Yes, Papa," she said. "I really miss you too."

Weeks after Reshma Mokenwar and Preethi Sarikela, a lesbian couple
from the southern Indian state of Telangana, are forced to separate by their
families, they elope to Mumbai with the help of human rights activists.
Reshma and Preethi find a community in a group of lesbian women
determined to break the cultural silence around homosexual desire even as
the Supreme Court debates the relevance of Section 377, a colonial-era law
that criminalizes homosexuality. But the city changes something between
them that can never be repaired.

Chapter 17

A Matter of Pride

"Hit it! Break it! Crush it!" Reshma Mokenwar shouted. She was bent over in her mother's kitchen in an oversize shirt and loose-fitting jersey shorts, holding her head as an offering. At the sink, Preethi Sarikela cried as she washed teacups. "Will that make you happy?" Reshma asked to meet her eye but Preethi refused to face her.

For four months, since Reshma had taken a kitchen knife and lopped off Preethi's hair in a mad rage, she had tried to rid Preethi of the spectral grip of that evening. At the hairdresser, for example, when Preethi cried at the sight of her shorn hair hanging unevenly over her ears, Reshma leaned in to whisper that her hair fall problem would finally disappear. When new hair came in, she knew from previous jobs assisting a doctor and working in a pharmacy, it would be thicker and shinier. On her birthday, Reshma gifted Preethi a pink lace gown and told her she would look exactly like a Barbie doll, but Preethi responded that since Barbie was not bald, she never needed to cover her head with scarves or beanies.

Until the night Reshma hacked Preethi's hair, they loved each other in a way that made their hearts dance and their bodies sing. Now when Reshma made love to her, she felt Preethi's body flop in defeat. Her lover was drifting away, lost in her sadness, possessed by the ghost of that evening. Preethi said the knife with which Reshma had cut her hair kept returning in her thoughts to cleave and tear into her until she was nothing but her severed plait.

As days passed, Preethi retreated into an impossible silence. Reshma did not know how to stop Preethi from disintegrating in front of her eyes, so she packed the life they were building together in plastic bags and moved them to her parents' house at Friends Colony in Bhandup. If Preethi was surrounded by voices outside her head, perhaps she would no longer hear the voices inside it.

The moment that Reshma threw Preethi's severed plait to the floor slapped Reshma awake to the sickening realization that, in some ways, she shared the worst traits of her father. The wild look of shock in Preethi's eyes was the same expression she had seen on her mother's face growing up. Like Babu Mokenwar, she was now discovering, Reshma Mokenwar had no practice with the emotion of guilt. She knew she had damaged the most important relationship of her life, and she wanted so badly to undo the hurt she had caused, but she could not bring herself to apologize. So she tried to flatter Preethi, as well as to coax her and fool her into forgetting that she was capable of cruelty. But she could not control the thoughts that came to Preethi when she was alone. Now, standing in her mother's kitchen, with her head in her hands, Reshma tried one more time to play Preethi into forgiving her. "All the time, 'My hair is gone, my hair is gone, my hair is gone!'" Reshma spat. "You have nothing else to cry about?"

◆━━━◇━━━◆

Across a low wall that separated the kitchen from the living area of her family's one-room home, Babu Mokenwar sat in a lawn chair and dunked a slice of bread in his sweet milk tea. He wore a starched checked shirt, dress pants, and a metal link watch. Reshma's mother, Rekha, sat at the door in a frayed nightgown and calmly combed her hair.

"Leave her!" Babu Mokenwar shouted to his daughter when his head started to spin from watching Reshma circle around Preethi. "I'll find you a hundred better girls. Smarter, richer, prettier, from the city."

Months earlier, Reshma's parents had given up on talking their daughter out of her sexual orientation. They trained their utilitarian minds to see her as nothing more than another source of household income. It no longer mattered to them whether she had sex with men or women, as long as she did not go around announcing it to neighbors in the chawl and her salary came in on time.

What filled them with loathing was the fact that of all the lesbians in the world, Reshma had chosen Preethi, the daughter of Babu Mokenwar's cousin sister Narsa, and turned their lives into a scandal in their village. Every now and then, murmurs from the village floated to the city and reminded them of the disgrace. Births, deaths, weddings, and festivals came and went, but the Mokenwars stayed put in the city, too fearful of facing relatives and friends in the countryside. They could not help themselves from treating Preethi poorly, in the hope that she would run back to the village, and the gossiping would finally stop.

"Look at the difference between them," Babu said, turning to his wife. "If our daughter is a hundred, is she even ten?"

"There is no comparison between them." Rekha slapped a palm of oil in her center parting.

In a loud voice, for Preethi to hear, Reshma's father said, "I have seen so many women from godforsaken villages come to the city with their heads covered in big, long veils. In two, three days, they are in jeans, wearing lipstick, carrying touch mobiles, looking tip-top. And *this* girl, been with Reshma for two, three years, knows nothing except how to cry, still looking like a fool from the village. Look at her: Can anyone say she is worthy of living in the city with our daughter in style?"

Rekha replied, "Even if a dog comes to the house, it eats a chapati you throw at it and goes away, wagging its tail in thanks. But this one? This one shows no sign of leaving. Worse than a dog also."

Reshma finally interrupted her parents, snapping, "Why will she go anywhere if I am here?" She turned to Preethi to see if speaking up on her behalf was impressive, but the young woman's head was bowed, and her tears hit the stone floor like fat raindrops.

Rekha said defensively, "All I keep saying to her is, 'Go and meet your parents; at least go once and tell everyone in the village that we are not in the wrong alone.' But she keeps on saying she will go after she has saved ten or twenty thousand rupees."

"Who will give you so much money?" Babu Mokenwar burst out laughing and spat out his water. "You don't even have hair on your head."

◆━━━◇━━━➤

A little after nine, Reshma sat in a corner of her parents' house, talking into her cell phone, waiting for Preethi to stop crying so that they could leave for work. Her mother had thrown a scarf over her nightgown and left to scrub dirty dishes in the marble-floored apartments of the high-rises surrounding the chawl. Her father had left for his driving job in the old part of the city.

Since they had moved to Bhandup, it had been made clear to Reshma and Preethi that they were a drain on the household, and if they wanted to stay, they would have to find a way to shoulder expenses. Reshma and Preethi started several businesses together because Reshma liked the idea of being their own bosses after working days and nights for a pittance at hotel jobs in Shirdi.

In their first week in the city, they sourced towels from a wholesale dealer and sold them from cane baskets at the crowded street corner near the train station. Their necks and backs burned in the scorching sun, but they barely recouped the cost of the towels. In their third week, Preethi had the idea to start a catering business selling *poha*, halva, noodles, and rice, but the venture had to be wrapped up within days of printing pamphlets because of territorial fights with Rekha over use of the kitchen stove at home.

At ten thirty, Reshma decided she could no longer wait for Preethi to finish crying, so she changed into a white shirt with a whistle attached to the shoulder flap to start a new job as a security guard in a nearby factory that manufactured fire extinguishers. She wanted Preethi to come along so they could find her a job at a printing press in the same industrial estate, but she was still inconsolable.

"Wash your face," Reshma said. "We are getting late."

"The choice is yours," Preethi said firmly. "Your mother or me."

This was not the first time Preethi had asked Reshma to choose between her and Rekha, but Reshma pretended to be shocked. Less because of what Preethi said and more because of the way she said it. Like an ultimatum.

"Are you threatening me?" Reshma asked.

"You can assume whatever suits you."

Everyone knew that Rekha and Preethi detested each other. Every now and then, Reshma tried to defuse the tension between them by begging her mother to tolerate Preethi. Reshma put her head in her mother's lap and said that if Rekha wanted her daughter to be happy, she would accept Preethi as a daughter-in-law. And every now and then, Reshma explained to Preethi that her mother was irritable because she was suffering from menopause. If she truly loved Reshma, she would accept Rekha as her mother-in-law.

Even before the fights started, the two women burned with a silent hatred for each other. Reshma had seen her mother's face turn pale when she saw Preethi standing beside her on their first day back in the city. Later, Reshma had found her mother grumbling to a photo of Lord Krishna that Preethi had cast a spell on her daughter and made her homosexual. Reshma had also seen how Preethi had suddenly created a scene, crying that she needed new slippers, when Reshma gave her mother four thousand rupees and a gold-plated Sai Baba poster from their joint savings. Preethi accused Reshma of spending all their money on her own mother and leaving nothing to send to her family in the village.

"Did you come here for my love or my money?" Reshma said when she understood the full significance of Preethi's threat.

"Your choice." Preethi looked her in the eye one more time. "Your mother or me."

◆──◆──◆

Some seventy-five years earlier, on August 8, 1942, Mohandas Karamchand Gandhi, the spiritual and political leader of India's freedom struggle, sat inside a cloth-and-bamboo pavilion at the Gowalia Tank Maidan, a park in an old part of Bombay, now Mumbai, and gave a speech that brought the country to the brink of independence.

"Here is a mantra, a short one, that I give to you. You may imprint it on your hearts and let every breath of yours give expression to it. The mantra is 'Do or die.' We shall either free India or die in the attempt; we shall not live to see the perpetuation of our slavery," Gandhi said to a thundering crowd.

Gandhi's "Do or die" became a rallying cry for the Quit India Movement that thundered across the length and breadth of the subcontinent. Mass protests calling for *azadi*—the word for freedom in Hindi, Urdu, Farsi, Bengali, Punjabi, and Kashmiri—erupted in villages and cities and culminated in the dismantling of British occupation five years later.

Decades after that speech, Reshma and Preethi stood in the same maidan in a crowd thumping to the call for queer *azadi* at the Mumbai Pride March. A young woman took the microphone. "We've finally won the Section 377 judgment, so hip hip hooray to all of us!" she declared. "I want to hear a really loud cheer because this is the first time we are meeting after the Section 377 judgment." A young *hijra*—a transgender person—swung into the center and started to dance as the crowd burst into chants of "Queer *azadi zindabad!*" "Long live queer freedom!"

The same ground that birthed India's freedom movement swelled with rainbow flags, drums, umbrellas, horns, crowns, feather boas, bow ties, pinwheels, bells, beauty queen sashes, and confetti in a celebration of another relic of colonial occupation being struck down. Like Gandhi, who used his body as a symbol of his politics, the maidan thundered with faces painted rainbow colors.

Reshma and Preethi, who had heard about the Mumbai Pride March from a post in A Free Life, the chat group of lesbian women, and decided to join to steal time away from the fights at home, found themselves swept up in the tidal wave of dance and laughter. Someone thrust a signboard in Preethi's hand that said, "Annihilate Patriarchy!" and she hoisted it over her head, her whole body shaking with laughter. For the first time in months, Preethi gave herself permission to laugh from the pit of her stomach. She danced, shrieked, sang, swung her hips, jumped, flailed her arms, and stuck out her tongue at the cameras. Reshma stood at a distance with her thumbs hooked in her jeans pockets and kept an eye out for perverts who infiltrated the crowd to rub up against women. It was hard work to not be dazzled by Preethi at a time like this, when she was lost in a kind of happy delirium. Even without her long hair, Reshma thought, Preethi was the most gorgeous woman in this whole city, especially when she glanced across the crowd to meet her gaze and threw her head back to laugh.

It was exactly for moments like these that Reshma had wanted them to leave Shirdi. That village was not noisy enough to absorb the bitter memories of their fights. She knew that if Preethi laughed so hard that it made her cry, she would heal. She would forget about the hair and the cruelty. Her own laughter would free her and return her to the present.

Before sunset, the Mumbai Pride March arrived in Azad Maidan, an open space containing twenty-two cricket pitches, across from a colonial railway station built to commemorate fifty years of Queen Victoria's rule. In 1931, on his return from the Second Round Table Conference in London, Gandhi stood in this maidan and told his followers to be prepared to sacrifice for freedom. "What I have to tell you now is that, if there is to be a fight, be prepared for every sacrifice, but take a pledge that you will not do harm to others," he said. "May God give us the strength to suffer and sacrifice in the cause of freedom."

Now a young man in a fluorescent green dress and heels stood at a mike and shouted, "I am gay!" He turned his ear to the crowd to hear it shout back, "That's okay!" Next, a woman grabbed the mike to declare, "I am lesbian!" and the crowd roared back, "That's okay!" A *dhol* player started pounding his double-sided barrel drum, and a software engineer dressed as a mythological Hindu king took a rainbow flag in his mouth and started to rotate his hips.

After sunset, even though Preethi was breathless from shouting and dancing, she did not want to go home to Bhandup, so they followed the crowd and wandered into a nightclub that hosted a party for Gay Pride. Walking inside, past men and women singing along to an English song with shocked faces, as if the words were passing through the bodies like electric currents, was nothing like entering a foul-smelling country liquor shop to extract a drunk brother or father.

When "Roop Tera Mastana," a sensual song from a 1969 blockbuster film titled *Aradhana*, started playing, Preethi pulled Reshma onto the dance floor, pushed up against her, and turned her face to look into her eyes. "Why are you like this?" Preethi said as she put her arms around Reshma's neck and did not expect an answer.

The next morning, when they stumbled home to Bhandup, Preethi placed a small rainbow flag over the low wall that separated the kitchen from the living area and started to make two cups of tea.

Reshma's mother stood in the doorway. "We thought we had finally got rid of you," she said sourly.

＊┄┄◇┄┄➤

Not a day passed in the Mokenwar household without small arguments escalating into dirty fights. Reshma knew she had to get Preethi out before she became totally consumed by the despair of living with her in-laws. If there was anyone in the family who could help them pay a deposit for a separate room, it was Kishen, the younger of her two brothers and the only member of the household with a good job, at a bank.

When Reshma was nine, she snuck out of the house to join a game of gully cricket. Kishen ran home to tattle that although Reshma had told her parents she was playing house-house with other girls, she had actually forced herself into a game meant for boys. As part of her punishment, their father instructed Kishen to drink his sister's share of sweet milk in front of her. Kishen looked up at Reshma, finished the milk in one long gulp, and licked his lips.

Years later, when she returned home after her divorce, it had often felt to Reshma that Kishen was her best friend. He was the only one in the family who did not treat her like a joke. When she fell for Preethi, he introduced her to Pooja and Poonam, a lesbian couple from his circle of friends. When Preethi's family refused to let her talk with Reshma, Kishen rallied friends in high places in the village and drew up plans for Reshma to get Preethi out of the house so they could elope. Even though the scheme did not materialize, Reshma was touched by the gesture. Whenever he shocked her with acts of kindness, Reshma liked to think that Lord Krishna, the deity of love after whom Kishen was named, was looking over her through her brother.

One afternoon, when Reshma walked in on Preethi and Kishen

laughing together, she started to suspect that her brother's kindness might be a figment of her imagination. The moment she entered the room, the two of them fell silent. She asked them what they had been talking about, but they offered a weak excuse of a lie. Kishen looked up at his sister and met her eye with the same defiance as the six-year-old boy who licked his lips after finishing her share of sweet milk.

It drove Reshma mad that Preethi followed Kishen around as if she were attached to him by an invisible leash. She always handed him a glass of water as soon as he came home from work, washed his clothes without being asked to, warmed his bathwater in time for him to leave for work, cooked his meals, and sat with him to give him company while he ate. Once, when Reshma saw Kishen roll a towel around his neck and glance across the room so Preethi could run out with a can of water for him to take to the common toilet outside, she slapped the water out of her hand.

"Will you wipe his shit for him also?" Reshma demanded.

"I talk to him because he is taking a loan for us," Preethi whispered.

"I don't like you talking to him," Reshma said. "You will not talk to him."

"Why?"

"You know my brother better than me?" Reshma shouted. "Why do you keep testing my patience?"

"What will you do now?" Preethi shouted back. "Cut my tongue off? Break my arms? Saw off my legs?"

Chapter 18

How to Say It

Late one monsoon evening in July 2020, Preethi Sarikela bathed and lay down to watch a Telugu soap opera after she had washed and dried the dishes, stacked the kitchen shelves, and wiped down the platform.

In a new episode of *Bangaru Panjaram*, a young bride climbed up on a stool and reached for copper vessels on the top shelf of her new kitchen. She wore a silk sari, delicate gold earrings, and the afterglow of a first wedding night. Her opulent hair, still wet from a bath, was tied loosely with a string of jasmine flowers. As she groped for a pan, she lost her footing and prepared to fall to a soundtrack of ringing temple bells. Before it could be revealed whether a husband appeared in the kitchen to break her fall and sweep her up in his arms or a mother-in-law sneered with malice, the scene was interrupted by the gloom of a life insurance commercial.

By the time the commercials ended, Preethi had drifted to sleep,

231

and the ringing temple bells had become part of her dream. She saw herself standing on her toes on the kitchen stool, wearing a gold-embroidered silk sari hitched up to one side, her blouse drenched from her long wet hair. She reached for the copper pots and pans on the top shelf and prepared to fall as the temple bells grew louder. She plummeted, delicately and beautifully, and landed in the arms that waited for her. When she saw that it was Reshma's brother Kishen who cradled her, drawing her close to trace the shape of her lips with his hungry eyes, she panicked and woke as suddenly as she had fallen asleep.

When her eyes opened, the room was dark and still. The lights were off, except for a flickering electric candle in the wall shrine that cast dancing shadows of the deities that crowded the wooden shelf. For a while, she lay awake with her thoughts, listening to the crash of milk crates, the blaring tunes of old Hindi songs from passing taxis, a drunk shouting abuse at a howling dog. Suddenly she felt an ache in the pit of her stomach. What was Kishen doing in her dream? How would she face Kishen and his fiancée, Rani, now that she had seen him this way? What about Reshma?

She turned to observe Reshma's sleeping face, to see what she looked like with her big eyes closed, to listen to her thoughts when her tongue was thick and unmoving, to study the shape of her small hands. Across the room, Reshma's father was splayed on his stomach on a cot, and her mother was curled up against the steel cupboard. Cloaked in darkness, their bodies looked weak and small, their cruelty worn out by the monotony of the daily rhythms of life.

If she could see Kishen properly once again, she decided, her stomachache would vanish. She would study his dirty fingernails, his furrowed forehead, his ragged beard, and confirm that he was not the man she had seen in her dream. She would stand up and announce that it was all a terrible misunderstanding, and everyone would nod drowsily in agreement and fall back to sleep. Then she would stretch out, sleep peacefully, and wake up like nothing happened.

In the darkness, when Preethi lifted herself up on an elbow, she finally saw Kishen in the glow of the dancing shadows, arm resting loosely over his eyes, strong and dark like a violin.

◆┈┈◇┈┈◆

The next morning, Preethi woke early and left for work at the printing press down the road. A row of heavy typesetting machines swallowed rolls of paper like hungry metal giants, and the smell of caramelized ink broke through the stench of printing solvents. Preethi sat by the window with a paper guillotine, slicing glossy card stock into advertisements for Park Avenue deodorant, and watched the street awaken gradually with the laughter of schoolgirls rushing out of a bus, the grunts of tea sellers trundling their carts to the footpath, and the grumbles of old women hobbling into a temple as a soft drizzle swayed in the wind.

A little after nine, in the middle of a sudden downpour, she saw a couple pull up on a scooter. They ran to take shelter under the thatched roof of a shuttered shop, the husband holding an office satchel over his wife, and the wife shielding a lunch bag under a fold of her sari. For a while, the couple stood close together, silently watching the rain crashing down in front of them. A song played in the distance, and the wife spread her arms out dramatically as if they were in a scene from a romantic film. The husband eyed her with amusement and gently pulled her close to adjust a string of jasmine flowers in her braid.

As she watched, Preethi felt a chill run through her. The shrieks of rain pooling at the floor of the city were the shrieks of a rebellion building inside her. This is what love was meant to look like. It was not supposed to be something to fear. It did not have to be beaten into you. It was not the sting of disrespect. It was not a state of quiet vengeance. It shielded you from rain and brought flowers to your hair. It did not bring knives to your head to cut your self-worth to shreds.

She wondered how life would have turned out if she were still with her high school boyfriend Shekar. When she left the village with Reshma, he had told her that he would wait for her. Could it be that he was still single three years later because he was really waiting for her?

For the rest of the week, when Preethi came home from work, she fell asleep without eating dinner. At night, when Reshma pressed up against her, she got up to drink water or go to the bathroom. Every morning, she left for work before Reshma woke.

"What *khichdi* is cooking inside your head?" Reshma stood at Preethi's work station at the printing press one afternoon. Preethi looked up and saw her partner growling and flapping like a character from the Angry Birds video game on her phone. Reshma's paunch slipped out of the khaki pants of her security guard uniform, her schoolboy hair flopped in the air, and her shrill voice trembled comically. Preethi felt embarrassed that everyone in the room assumed that the angry bird was her life partner.

"Why did you come here?" Preethi whispered as the printing needle danced on an unfurling bolt of paper. "I told you not to come here."

"Why?" Reshma shouted back. "You are ashamed of me? You don't want your friends to see your life partner?"

Even though it was nearly impossible to hear over the grunts and gurgles of the printers, Preethi was sure she heard laughter dribble across the room.

"You go now." Preethi walked Reshma to the door. "We will talk when I come home."

◆┄┄◇┄┄➤

After ten, Preethi and Reshma walked in silence in the direction of darkness, through the winding lanes of the chawl, away from the echoing wails of women in the prime-time soap opera, beyond rows of saris wrung out to dry, past young men walking in packs smoking and talking, until they reached the deserted steps of an old school.

Preethi waited for the street to empty out and turned to Reshma with tears streaming down her face. She said she did not know how to say it but she had to say it. There was no right way to say it, but it was wrong to not say it. This was all a terrible mistake.

Reshma's confused face suddenly softened with laughter. She took Preethi's hand and told her that she did not like fighting either. She knew she often lost her temper, and Preethi bore the brunt of it, but it was only because she was the one person in the world who was her own. If only Preethi could allow Reshma's anger to pass, know-ing that underneath her actions were the hurt feelings of a good person who loved her, they would never fight again. Where else was Reshma supposed to go? Who else could she be real with? Preethi was Reshma's Chinni, she said. Sweet like sugar. She was her Bacha, she said. A baby girl.

Preethi stood up, looked her in the eyes, and told her to stop talking. She said that she could no longer play along and tell her she loved her, because her heart was drained empty. A strange feeling had grown in her stomach and robbed her of her peace. She had found herself admiring the hands of men. She had fantasized about being touched by them. She had hoped it was a passing feeling, but days had turned into weeks, and the feeling had stayed and festered into a peculiar sorrow that had lodged itself in her skin.

Now she longed to be married to a man. She dreamed about having children and starting a family of her own. She wanted to have an ordinary life. She did not want to fight her family. She wanted to visit her parents with her husband and children and celebrate festivals and eat and dance and laugh together. She wanted to live with respect. She had nothing against Reshma. This was no one's fault. It was preordained by the bodies they were born into. She was sorry. She was exhausted from fighting with herself. Sometimes she thought about putting an end to her life to put an end to the agony.

"You are ashamed because I am a woman?" Reshma said. "You know I will do anything for you. I will become a man for you. Trust me. I will become a man for you."

◆┅┅◇┅┅➤

"Good morning, sir." Reshma sent a private message to the social media accounts of Aryan Pasha, a celebrity bodybuilder who had transitioned to the male gender with a sex-reassignment surgery. "I want to do trans, please help me. I want to do it at any cost," she wrote.

"Because I want that when people see my life partner with me, they don't laugh. They don't taunt her. They give her respect," Reshma wrote to professors of women's studies at the Tata Institute of Social Sciences.

To a newspaper journalist, she proposed, "I know I will need millions of rupees for the operation. I need good people who can make an investment in me. They should not worry about money right now. Later, when I do something in my life, they will get rich and famous with me. But it should be fast, before my partner leaves me."

"I am scared she will leave me because of the mother-pricks sister-pricks who keep laughing at her and asking how she can waste her life with me," she wrote to a friend. "Especially the pricks I call my brothers, Kishen and Ganesh, think that women are the dirt on their shoes."

"What if she leaves me to get married, and my soul keeps on suffering and wandering behind her?" she wrote to the assistant of a Tantrist who cured love problems with her magical powers.

Despite the tumult within her, Reshma maintained a slow, deceptive calm around Preethi. She agreed to book train tickets when Preethi insisted on going home to see her parents. She suppressed the urge to raise her voice when Preethi refused to wait to travel until after restrictions for the coronavirus pandemic were lifted. Reshma smiled and nodded even though Preethi's stubbornness and defiance grated against her skin. She kept her cool even when she read messages Preethi had sent to her old boyfriend from the village. "Hi," Preethi wrote. "How are you?" Reshma wanted to shake Preethi and ask how it was possible to suddenly stop loving someone. *Why did she send those messages to Shekar? Why did she want to talk to him after all these years? Why did she care how he was? Why was she thinking of him? Was this not a form of betrayal?* The questions followed Reshma around like a ghostly echo, but she did not allow herself to ask them. If she asked now, she knew, Preethi would leave and never come back.

Late one afternoon, when Kishen stumbled home from work earlier than usual, swaying, swinging, and stinking, Reshma absentmindedly instructed Preethi to unfurl a straw mat for him to sleep off the effects of whatever poison he had gotten drunk on. As he stretched out, Reshma saw Kishen grab Preethi's hand, pull her close, and tap his cheek, gesturing for a kiss.

⬦ ⬦ ⬦

What followed was a blur of frozen moments. Reshma's shining, crooked teeth. A leather belt dangling in her hand. The sting of the belt striking Preethi's legs and back like red-hot kitchen tongs. The screams of Kishen's fiancée, Rani, when she saw Preethi empty a bottle of nail polish in her mouth. The taste of fumes. A surge of salt water filling Preethi's mouth. Rani thumping her back to force Preethi to vomit. The image of Preethi looking at herself in the bathroom mirror, face slick with sweat, hair disheveled, eyes swollen.

⬦ ⬦ ⬦

For most of August, Preethi had trouble sleeping. She would dream of herself tearing through the Friends Colony's curving narrow lanes, dodging cars on the vast highways leaving Bhandup, and landing in a window seat of an overnight bus to Adilabad, sinking back, laughing, yawning, stretching, the stiffness of her bones melting away. She would dream of waking up as she flew past barren fields to Bazarhathnoor, waiting for the Hanuman Temple to loom into view, and walking past a row of powder-pink houses, waving at neighbors. She would see herself throwing her purse on the bed, pouring herself a glass of water, and asking her mother what happened in the new episode of *Bangaru Panjaram*.

The day Preethi really left, she did not tell anyone. By late evening, when she still had not returned home from work, Reshma went looking for her. The printing press was closed. Her phone was switched off. No one had seen her at the bus station or the rickshaw stand. Until the last train left, Reshma ran up and down the railway platform, screaming her name, howling, sitting down, getting up, searching train compartments, looking into windows, biting her lips, punching the wall to punish the hands that had struck Preethi with a belt, crying into her elbow, slamming the doors of empty bathrooms, flashing photos of Preethi to strangers, shrieking and tearing through the crowd, not knowing which way to go.

At midnight, when Kishen called to say that Preethi had collected the rest of her salary at work that morning and that her parents were expecting her in Bazarhathnoor, Reshma realized that the love of her life was really gone. She wandered down the empty railroad, along rows of decommissioned tracks, and sat down on a dry riverbed covered in sewage, frayed plastic, old slippers, scraps of cardboard, bottle caps—tributaries of human waste. She looked up at the sky and saw the skeletons of cotton stalks swaying in a pale moonlight from a night seven years ago, when she had picked up a bottle of pesticide to escape her husband and the torture of living with him.

◆┄┄┄◇┄┄┄▶

Two months later, in October 2020, Reshma woke up on the floor of a stranger's home. The night Preethi left, strangers found Reshma sitting on the railroad tracks and dragged her to safety on the platform. Someone gave her a bottle of water and told her to be grateful for another chance at life. She walked home to the Friends Colony, burst into her parents' house, and threw herself at her father, kicking and screaming, blaming him for sending Preethi away. Reshma then asked for money so she could get sex-reassignment surgery and demanded to be addressed as a man. Reshma's father slapped her, broke her phone in two, and threw her out of the house. From that moment on, Reshma adopted gender-free pronouns.

Reshma wandered through a nearby slum with nothing except the clothes on their back until a Tantric guru who wore chiffon saris and talked to spirits took them in. The god-woman, who called herself Amma and specialized in providing relief from enemies, allowed Reshma to sweep and mop her hut in exchange for a place to sleep.

Late one evening, Reshma cooked dinner as Amma sat hypnotized in front of a Hindi soap opera. During a sanitary napkin commercial, she turned to the kitchen and asked Reshma why they wanted to change the gender they were born into for a love that was long gone.

"Because when I was in a woman's body, she was ashamed of me. She used to get angry even if I walked next to her. She used to cry when her friends came with their husbands. She used to turn away when I touched her. She used to dream of being touched by men. She told me herself.

"See, it will cost five lakhs for the sex change surgery." Seven thousand dollars. "How will I get so much money? I don't know how I will get the money, but I know I have no other option but to get it. If I stop working and start to sell my body—by that, I mean if I have sex for a hundred rupees or two hundred rupees per customer, and if I take five or six customers every night, if I let those men climb on top of me and do whatever they want to do, I will make money. But it will still take fifteen or twenty years to save five lakhs, which is the amount I need to become a man. I am willing to do that. I am willing to get raped a thousand times every night. For a chance to become a man and for a chance to be with Preethi. I will do it. Again and again."

Reshma gasped for breath. "I know that by then, Preethi may be married, and she may also have her own children. That is okay with me. Let her marry. Let her have children. You know why? Because I am her first love.

"Even if I am fifty by the time I become a man, I will go to her village, I will buy a house next to her house, I will look very good. I will wear good clothes, and I will be tip-top. All I will have to do is take her hand. I have full faith. I know that the minute I touch her hand, she will come with me. The minute I touch her, she will leave her husband and children, and she will walk with me. She will just walk and walk. Her anger will melt away. She won't look back. You know why? Because I am her first love."

A Note on Sources

The stories in this book are a result of hundreds of hours of interviews that took place over half a decade during which most of the pivotal events described took place. I interviewed Sanjoy Sachdev, Paji Saheb, and Vilas Dongre with the same rigor as the young couples and their families. I spoke to more than a hundred and fifty people between 2016 and 2021 and all of those interviews were recorded on tape. When it became impossible to tape, such as when a police officer objected to recording a conversation between himself and Dawinder's father Gurmej Singh, I took handwritten notes and emailed myself to describe the mood of the interview later that day. The facts in this book are corroborated with court records, first information reports, official documents, and forensic results that I gathered from courthouses in Nagpur, Chandigarh, New Delhi, and Mumbai. They are also supplemented with news reports, videos, and chat transcripts.

I was present for most of the events described at the Love Commandos shelter. The dialogue took place in front of me and was recorded on tape. When I use quotation marks to describe Neetu's thought process, the source is either an interview with her or her personal diary. The description of the attack on Sukhwinder Kaur was reconstructed from interviews with the family, neighbors, police officers, and first information reports. I saw the destruction of the house for myself when I travelled to the village days later. I was present when Gurmej Singh approached Jitender Kumar, the police inspector at Siwan Police Station.

I interviewed Monika and Arif in every city in which they lived. When I describe conversations between Arif and Monika in quotations, they are either sourced from chat transcripts between them over Facebook Messenger or retold to me in later interviews. The impressions of Bhagyashri are based on interviews with Arif, Monika, their families, cousins, and common friends. The conversation between Bhagyashri and Tabssum after Monika and Arif's disappearance was conveyed to me by Tabssum and corroborated by Bashir and Khaled, who were present in the room when the call was allegedly answered on speaker phone. The scene describing the attack on Akida Khemani's home was reconstructed from extensive interviews with the family and neighbors from Hasanbagh. Akida's teenage daughter Muskan was especially helpful, providing photos, videos, and copies of news reports that appeared in local papers. Vilas Dongre's interviews with the press that I quote from were with the Marathi-language news channels including Saam TV and TV9. The interview with Yogi Adityanath that aired on Aap Ki Adalat is linked in the endnotes.

I witnessed many of the events described in Reshma and Preethi's story, such as the scene at Reshma's home where Preethi is compared to a dog or when Reshma is thrown out of her home. In some cases, I reported the events shortly after they occurred, such as when Preethi's hair was lopped off. After the summer of 2020, when Preethi left Reshma and returned to Bazarhathnoor, we stayed in touch over the phone.

The young men and women I met in the beginning of the project grew up over the course of reporting it. Their ideas about themselves and their place in the world often changed. Their desires and dreams evolved. Their loyalties and affections shifted. In the preceding pages, I have tried my best to portray the full complexity of their individual truths. No names have been changed.

Afterword

One monsoon afternoon in 1973, when my mother was seventeen, she stole away from college to watch a matinee show of the 1960 movie *Mughal-e-Azam* with my father. The story is set in the reign of the sixteenth-century Mughal emperor Akbar and based on the legend of Salim and Anarkali, the Mughal crown prince and a dancing girl. Prince Salim and Anarkali's love, forbidden by the social taboos around nobility and class, comes to a tragic end when Emperor Akbar orders Anarkali to be buried alive.

My mother, the daughter of a wealthy merchant, was in love with my father, a struggling engineer from the chawls. They wanted to marry with their families' permission, but they knew it was impossible, so they allowed the fantasy of the dancing girl and the crown prince to fall over them like a warm blanket and lull them to sleep.

Six decades after the film was released, *Mughal-e-Azam* is still the grandest national model of doomed romance. Every now and

then, a new film, television show, or musical attempts a retelling of
the legend because a glorious forbidden love is as relevant to young
people now as it was to young people then.

We keep returning to Salim and Anarkali because we try to see
ourselves in the prince and the dancing girl whose great love was
sabotaged by the tyranny of social strictures. We draw moral power
from the story of Salim and Anarkali because it assigns a greater
meaning to our choices. It teaches us that life is too small to contain
the enormity of love. It reminds us that whenever great love visits, it
leaves behind a world thrown apart by it.

◆┄┄┄◇┄┄┄▶

I reported *The Newlyweds* over the course of six years, spending long
stretches of time in Mumbai, New Delhi, Kakheri, Karnal, Rohtak,
Chandigarh, Nagpur, Basmath, Shirdi, Nanded, Beed, Akola, Hy-
derabad, Bhopal, and Adilabad. The facts in these stories have been
corroborated through police reports, court files, transcripts of chat
and text messages, videos, and photos.

Over the course of reporting, I witnessed Neetu and Dawinder
grow up, Arif and Monika grow in love, and Reshma and Preethi
grow apart. I came to learn that growing can look a lot like suffering, and it happens when our expectations and reality collide. "Love
is like a sandalwood tree," Arif's grandmother Momina told me one
afternoon in her hometown of Basmath. "Even after you cut down
the tree to a pile of stumps, you can smell it in the air."

◆┄┄┄◇┄┄┄▶

In April 2019 Arif heard that Monika's sister, Bhagyashri, had moved to
Mumbai for a new posting as a police constable. The news tore through

the fragile sense of security he had woven out of unsaid assurances over the months Monika had been talking to her father on the phone. "He has come," Monika whispered whenever she heard Arif walk through the door. "Should we talk later?" Then she would scramble to hang up.

One evening, as Monika heaped their dinner plates with biryani, Arif cleared his throat. For weeks, he had suppressed the urge to ask Monika what she and her father talked about because he felt afraid of learning too much. Suddenly the news of Bhagyashri moving to Mumbai filled him with a sense of feeble urgency.

"How is everyone at home?" he asked.

"Fine."

"Bhaga is in Mumbai," he said.

"I know."

"You do?"

"Papa wants her to bring me back home to Nagpur," she said. "He says, 'Forget everything and come back to your own house.'"

"What did you tell him?" Arif's eyes welled up.

"I told him my house is here with you and our daughter."

After the birth of Neetu and Dawinder's son, Gunveer, in October 2017, the family moved into a room down the street from Kulwant Kaur's bungalow. Even though Neetu tried to make the new house her own by organizing kitchen shelves the way she liked them, scattering her powders and creams on the dresser, and hanging the life-size poster of herself that lay in the bottom of her suitcase, she felt a type of loss. Her days vanished into the loneliness of caring for a newborn, and Dawinder's new job at a scaffolding and shuttering company left him exhausted and irritable.

"When we had time, we didn't have each other," Neetu told me one afternoon in May 2020 over a video call. They had called to share the news that Dawinder had been promoted at work. "Now we have each other, but we don't have time."

When Neetu ran out of the frame to show me a *sherwani* she had stitched for Gunveer's birthday, Dawinder told me that he had been thinking about applying for construction jobs abroad to earn back what his family had lost because of their elopement and marriage. The house in Kakheri was still unsold, and savings from the sale of ancestral land were being drained by lawyers' fees to continue the fight for compensation from Neetu's family. "When we were young, we cared about no one but ourselves," Dawinder reflected. "We thought only about our love, our problems, our desires, our lives."

Moments later, when Neetu returned with the *sherwani*, humming a Punjabi love song, she screwed up her face. "'My eyes wish they never stop looking at you'"? She recited the lyrics of the song as if she had just heard them. "Who writes such absurd songs?"

For nearly a year after Preethi moved back with her parents, Reshma tried to get her to respond to their calls and messages. They flooded her phone and social media with proof of remorse: videos of themselves crying, photos of their cut-up wrist, love songs. When nothing worked, they posted intimate photos of them together in the hope that Preethi would be tempted to call them back in a flare of anger, but days turned into weeks, and Preethi's silence became impermeable.

"I am changing my name to Preethish," they wrote to Preethi in text messages that were never delivered. "Do you like it?"

"I am sorry," Reshma wrote into the void. "I have made many mistakes."

"Are you sure you will be able to live without me?" Reshma wrote when they heard that Preethi's parents were looking for a groom. "I am sure you will not."

In June 2021 Reshma's extended family traveled to a village in Adilabad to attend Preethi's marriage to her cross-cousin Shekar. After the religious ceremony, Preethi and Shekar posed for a couple's photo shoot, dressed in the regalia of a medieval king and queen. Preethi wore a gold sari embellished with semiprecious stones, and Shekar wore a matching *sherwani* and turban.

In Mumbai, heavy monsoon rain pummeled the city. Streets flooded, trees fell, bridges collapsed, homes crumbled, and desperate crowds waded through waist-high water. "When a heart full of love breaks, a thunderstorm starts," Reshma texted me that evening with a selfie of them drenched in the rain.

＊━━◇━━＊

Every monsoon afternoon during the year I was eleven, I watched my mother's stomach swell and shrink beneath her floral nightgown as she slept beside me. The fan spun in a plastic sky that had been propped up with bamboo sticks to protect us from being awakened by the leaking ceiling. During those days, I was deeply disturbed that I was losing resemblance to my mother. She was short; I was already as tall as her. Her hair was straight and silken; mine was unruly. Her hands were round; mine were square.

I had never met my father, who left us after I was born and died shortly after, but I was told I inherited his appearance. For most of my childhood, I prayed with utter humility that I start to look like my mother. It would mean I was more like her than him, mainly so that I would not feel like a stranger to myself. When she slept, I felt that I could look at her more easily to search for myself in her face.

When my mother ran errands after work, she usually left my sister and me waiting in her blue Fiat to ward off tow trucks. One evening that monsoon, she took us upstairs to a house where an old man sat in an undershirt and sarong in a tattered sofa. He introduced himself as our grandfather and handed me a photo of a man wearing caramel-brown bell-bottoms and a patterned silk shirt. My father stood with one hand on his waist and one leg on a footstool, the way colonial hunters posed with wild animals killed in trophy expeditions. The man had short curly hair, a pencil-thin mustache, and my nose.

On the way home, when my mother popped her head out at the traffic light to adjust the broken car wiper and clear the windscreen with a hand towel, I thought about asking her why she decided to take us upstairs. When we reached home, I no longer wanted to know. I slipped the photograph of my father in an envelope and forgot where I hid it.

Acknowledgments

My deepest gratitude is to the men and women who let me into their lives. I am also indebted to the following people and institutions for their support, insights, and encouragement:

In India—Jagmati Sangwan, Alka Dhupkar, Pooja Nair, Kirti Singh, Jaideep Bose, Ranjana Kumari, Sanjana Chowhan, Pronoti Datta, Vaibhav Vats, Aviral Virk, Bhavatosh Singh, Nidhi Chopra, Mitali and Karan Sahani, Upasana Tayal, Gayatri Kaul, and Varun Jhangiani.

In the United States and elsewhere—Divya Mahadevia, Aarti Mirchandani, Divya Mahindra, Alexandra Katsoulis, Sadef Ali Kully, Kim Wall, Alexis Okeowo, Jordi Oliveres, Betsy Morais, Vauhini Vara, Annie Hylton, Jina Moore, Wendy Call, Suketu Mehta, Francesca Mari, Kit Rachlis, Vivek Nemana, Lauren Bohn, Helen Benedict, Nakul Roy, Sandra Garcia, Ellen Barry, Dhiya Kuriakose, Matthew Claiborne, Seth Maxon, Tekendra Parmar,

Basharat Peer, Rachel Poser, Sarah De Guzman Cayetano, Bimala Bhushal, International Women's Media Foundation, and New York University's Arthur L. Carter Journalism Institute.

The book *Manoj and Babli: A Hate Story*, by Chander Suta Dogra, and the documentary film *Izzatnagri Ki Asabhya Betiyan: The Immoral Daughters in the Land of Honor*, by Nakul Singh Sawhney, informed my writing. I am grateful to Tanish Malji and Sonakshi Bhandari for conceptualizing the cover design.

I am indebted to my agent, Jin Auh, who has been my champion from the day we first met. My editor, Amar Deol, who read every single version of every single draft and made it better each time. I am also thankful to Philip Bashe, for his thorough fact-checking and copyediting.

My family, Lachmi Wadhwa, Shobha and Raj Rajpal, Tarana and Vishal Masand, Ravina and Vinay Rajpal, and my nieces Samara, Aleya, Elisha, and Reyna. My late grandparents Vasumati and Suryakant Shah, Virumati Shah, Atul and Ketki Shah, and my sister, Parita Choksi. My mother, Zarana Choksi, my moral compass, who has taught me more than she will ever know. My husband, Suhail Rajpal, and our son, Kabir. They are the best part of me.

Credits

A version of Neetu and Dawinder's story was first published as "The New-lyweds" in the January 2018 issue of *Harper's*. It has been revised from its previously published version.

INDEX

About the Author

Mansi Choksi is a graduate of the Columbia School of Journalism and a two-time Livingston Award finalist. Her writing has appeared in the *New York Times*, the *New Yorker*, *Harper's*, *National Geographic*, the *Atlantic*, and more. She lives in Dubai with her husband and son. *The Newlyweds* is her first book.